Continental Accord:
North American Economic
Integration

Continental Accord: North American Economic Integration

Edited by Steven Globerman

The Fraser Institute
Vancouver, British Columbia, Canada

Canadian Cataloguing in Publication Data

Main entry under title:

Continental accord

Includes bibliographic references.
ISBN 0-88975-133-1

    1. Free trade—Canada. 2. Free trade—United States. 3. Free trade—Mexico. 4. North America—Economic integration. I. Globerman, Steven. II. Fraser Institute (Vancouver, B.C.)
HF1766.C65 1991   382'.97107   C91-091271-8

Printed in Canada.

Contents

Introduction

The central preoccupation of the Fraser Institute and its research program is the solutions that markets provide for the economic problems that are mankind's constant companion. This research constantly encounters barriers to market operation which are imposed by government actions of one kind or another. While often enacted with the best of intentions, these impediments frequently injure those they are intended to help and benefit groups who in turn become the champions of the political support for the impediments. Protectionism is undoubtedly one of the more insidious of these anti-market devices. The beneficiaries of protection are often concentrated politically, highly motivated by substantial gains, and effective in pressing their case. The victims of protectionism—consumers of the protected product—are diffuse in their interest, unaware or unconcerned about their loss and disorganized in pressing their own interests in the matter. Because of this asymmetry, protectionism is often the outcome of political action and has been a constant source of economic loss.

This book describes the economic gains that may be achieved by Canada, the United States and Mexico as a consequence of the willingness of these three countries to remove, in a mutually satisfactory way, the barriers to the operation of markets that have been erected in response to political pressures. It is the first stage in an extensive program of research and other activities which the Fraser Institute has undertaken in conjunction with the Centre for International Studies at the University of Toronto, the Americas Program at Stanford University, the Hudson Institute, the Center for Strategic and International Studies, Political Economy Research Center, El Colegio de Mexico, and economists at many of the most prestigious universities on the continent. This four-year program of activity has been generously funded by the Lilly Endowment, Inc. of Indianapolis and we are pleased to acknowledge their wholehearted support and the encouragement and insights that have been provided by John Mutz and Gordon St. Angelo.

There can be no more important set of issues than those that relate to the establishment of one market for most products on the North American continent. The Fraser Institute has therefore been pleased to lend its support and assistance to the accomplishment of this program of research which reaches out for an understanding of how North America will be configured as we begin to recognize the opportunities of the next century. However, the authors in this book and in all of the other projects in the program of the Fraser Institute work independently and are subject to review only by independent referees and editors. In consequence, the conclusions to which they come are their own and may or may not reflect the view of the members or the Trustees of the Fraser Institute.

Michael A. Walker

Preface

In February 1991, Canada, the United States, and Mexico agreed to negotiate a free trade agreement. Formal negotiations are expected to start in the spring of 1991. While it is unclear how long the negotiations will take, Mexico's Trade Secretary Jaime Serra Puche recently expressed the view that it was realistic to expect a first draft of the treaty by the end of 1991.[1] Against the background of strong political support given the initiative by Mexican President Salinas and U.S. President Bush, the end of 1991 might indeed appear to be a realistic date for a draft treaty; however, notwithstanding equally strong support given the Canada-U.S. free trade negotiations by then President Reagan and Prime Minister Mulroney, bilateral negotiations were protracted, sometimes stormy, and in the end were salvaged only in the final days before "fast track" provisions governing congressional ratification procedures for the agreement were about to expire. In short, one should not necessarily expect the voyage to trilateral free trade to be a smooth and rapid one.

A host of uncertainties and risks surround the negotiation process, especially at this early stage. One major uncertainty is how any resulting trilateral agreement will be harmonized with the existing Canada-U.S. Free Trade Agreement (FTA). Canada has indicated that it would object to any changes to the FTA that were perceived as unfavourable to Canada. For their part, both Mexico and the United States expressed concern in preliminary negotiations that the inclusion of Canada in trade talks might significantly slow Mexico-U.S. efforts at bilateral trade liberalization. A second and related uncertainty is the scope of any ensuing agreement and its precise terms. In the case of the FTA, a range of issues were left for future negotiations including several of the most controversial such as countervail and anti-dumping rules. It might be expected that any trilateral agreement pursuant to the upcoming round of negotiations will also leave a host of issues for future discussion.

North American free trade negotiations are taking place at a critical time in world trade developments. The recent Uruguay Round of the GATT negotiations ended in stalemate over several issues including agricultural subsidies. While there are currently ongoing efforts to revive the GATT negotiations, it can be argued that multilateral trade liberalization efforts have now taken a distinct back seat to regional trade liberalization initiatives. Indeed, regional trade agreements have become increasingly prominent over the past two decades. The European Community is perhaps the most important example,

---

1   See John Saunders, "3-way trade talks set," *Globe and Mail*, February 6, 1991, B1.

although the FTA and the Closer Economic Relations agreement between Australia and New Zealand constitute other illustrations. The de facto integration of the ASEAN economies around Japanese foreign direct investment represents still another development underscoring this trend towards regionalism.

Without necessarily being supporters of regional integration, many observers cite this trend as reinforcing a need to resolve North American trade issues, including those which remain outstanding under the FTA.[2] As will be made clear in this volume, there are still many significant barriers to free trade between Canada, Mexico, and the United States. Indeed, the current extent of economic integration in North America is modest compared to the ambitious program laid out for the European Community by 1992 or even the Australia-New Zealand experience under the Closer Economic Relations.

In these preliminary stages of discussion, participants in the upcoming North American debate are already staking out positions. In Canada and the United States, labour representatives have raised the spectre of massive unemployment being caused by an exodus of jobs to "low-wage" Mexican industries. Interestingly, labour leaders in Mexico have also raised cautions about preserving Mexican jobs in competition with capital and technology-intensive businesses located in the United States and Canada. Both Mexican and Canadian nationalists continue to worry about the political and cultural sovereignty of their countries in a free trade environment with the United States. Issues of sovereignty with respect to energy and water resources also surround the prospect of North American economic integration, as do potential issues of labour and capital mobility.

On the other hand, proponents of North American economic integration identify a broad range of economic and non-economic benefits. For example, Mexican supporters highlight the likely in-flows of much needed capital investment and technology. They also point to the indirect boost that faster Mexican growth will provide to the Canadian and U.S. economies. American supporters also stress the advantages of a faster growing Mexican economy to American exports and efforts to stem illegal migration from Mexico to the United States. Canadian supporters emphasize the need for Canada to remain inside any regional trade bloc encompassing its largest market, the United States. For Canada, a country of approximately 25 million people, a trilateral free trade agreement would put it securely inside a market consisting of some

---

2   See James Rusk, "Focus Shifting to FTA," *Globe and Mail*, December 13, 1990, B3.

360 million people with a total gross national product of around $6 trillion. This would make for a free trade area larger than the European Community.

Ultimately, the argument for free trade rests upon the principle that it contributes to higher standards of living within the free trade area. This basic principle has been enunciated by economists for hundreds of years and has been supported by countless empirical studies. To be sure, the inclusion of a country (Mexico) with a much lower real income level than its partners (Canada and the United States) in a free trade area is atypical of historical experience. For example, while Portugal and Spain were significantly poorer than their European Community partners, the difference was arguably not as marked as in the trilateral comparison. This difference in real standards of living along with related differences in the emphasis placed on economic versus non-economic public policy goals will likely feature prominently in the public debate surrounding trilateral trade negotiations. As well, it underscores the importance of careful research on the likely impacts of a North American free trade area.

The conventional wisdom that free trade leads to higher real incomes is likely to be sustained by a trilateral free trade agreement. Both theory and evidence suggesting that the removal of restrictions on international trade and investment is a powerful force for wealth creation are quite robust. However, the dislocations caused by the formation of a trilateral free trade area, encompassing Mexico, may be significant for specific sectors of the Canadian and U.S. economies. Once again, careful research is required to shed light on what will undoubtedly be a highly controversial issue in the ensuing debate.

The broad social and political consequences of trilateral trade liberalization will also be important issues in the free trade debate, as they were in the Canadian debate surrounding the FTA. Already opponents of trilateral free trade are raising prospects for the "subjugation" of the political and social "sovereignty" of the smaller trading partners by the United States; however, the experience of the European Community suggests that the political influence of the smaller countries was enhanced by joining the community. Nevertheless, one can expect issues such as the possible harmonization of tax legislation and environmental and social policies to be quite contentious, as indeed they were in the public debate surrounding the FTA.

Whatever the outcome of the current North American free trade discussions, it seems reasonable to assume that the issue of North American economic integration will remain important for the foreseeable future. With this prospect in mind, the Fraser Institute is undertaking a long-term study of various economic, political, and social issues surrounding North American economic integration. The overall project is entitled The Economic Future of North America. The motivation for the project is the Fraser Institute's conviction that as we move into the twenty-first century, closer economic relations among the

North American trading partners are increasingly important to both the economic and non-economic well-being of the respective countries. Hopefully, relatively early into the next century, the North American economies will have successfully implemented a program of economic integration at least as ambitious as the European Community has set out for itself.

This volume represents the first publication of research undertaken under the auspices of the project. It offers a broad perspective on the issues surrounding North American economic integration, taking vantage points from Mexico, Canada, and the United States. Taken as a whole, the volume highlights a set of arguments for North American economic integration along with an assessment of the potential problems in achieving closer economic relations. It should be noted that while the authors do not address all the relevant issues in a definitive way, they do identify the important issues surrounding the public debate and offer educated insights into the theoretical and practical relevance of the various arguments on both sides of the debate. The Fraser Institute will be releasing other studies over the next few years, through publications, conferences, and colloquia, which will address in much greater detail many of the issues raised in this volume.

The first chapter was prepared by Dr. Rogelio Ramirez de la O. He discusses why a North American free trade agreement encompassing the mobility of capital is vital to Mexico's efforts to switch from an import-protectionist stance to an export-led growth regime. He identifies the likely increases in Mexico's growth rate pursuant to a free trade agreement along with the likely expansion of Mexican imports and exports. His results support a view that the resulting faster growth rate in Mexico will benefit the economies of Mexico's North American trading partners. An openness to foreign capital investment and stable and predictable monetary and fiscal policies should mitigate any dislocations that will attend the continued liberalization of Mexico's trade regime with the United States and Canada.

The second chapter, written by Professor Leonard Waverman, offers a Canadian perspective on trilateral economic integration. Waverman evaluates the option of Canada joining a North American free trade agreement against the option of remaining outside such an agreement and watching Mexico and the United States conclude an agreement. He argues that Canada would clearly be economically and politically worse off under the second option. In particular, Canada would be even more disadvantaged in terms of competing against Mexican exporters in the U.S. market, while Canadian exporters would be at a disadvantage in competing against U.S. firms for sales in a rapidly growing Mexican market. At the same time, Canada's political "leverage" in a North American context would be enhanced by making "common ground" with

Mexico in a trilateral trade agreement. In short, remaining outside a trilateral trade agreement would saddle Canada with many costs and few benefits. The third chapter, by Dr. Clark Reynolds, offers a U.S. perspective on North American economic integration. Reynolds suggests that current economic conditions in the United States embody the recessionary effects of both weak domestic demand and a lack of international competitiveness on the part of many U.S. businesses. The latter is identified as "structural" recession and is associated with disinvestment and worker lay-offs in broad segments of the U.S. economy. Hence, there is a short-term need to boost capital investment in order to stimulate domestic demand, as well as a long-term need in order to facilitate structural readjustment of U.S. industries. He asserts that a trade agreement with Mexico will promote investment opportunities in U.S. industries, especially those exporting capital goods, thereby promoting both short-term and long-term policy objectives.

Reynolds cites other advantages to a North American free trade agreement. In particular, the current breakdown of GATT negotiations and the growth of European and Asian trading blocs make it more important to work on eliminating regional barriers to international business in North America. The Gulf Crisis highlights the importance of regional stability and energy security in U.S. public policy. Free trade with Mexico could well promote both objectives, particularly as it should promote much higher real incomes in Mexico which, in turn, should be a force for stabilization in the region. He acknowledges the potential for low-cost Mexican goods to displace U.S. production in low-skill labour intensive activities; however, the magnitude of this phenomenon will arguably be mitigated by rapid growth of the North American economies and by an aging population in the U.S. which could, in the foreseeable future, lead to labour shortages in the U.S. As well, with free trade there could be a decline in the "direct" importation of Mexican labour into the U.S., although continued Mexican immigration (perhaps at reduced levels) into the U.S. is both likely and desirable in a post-free trade environment.

In the fourth chapter, Professor Richard Lipsey examines the broad case for a trilateral free trade agreement against the alternative prospect of a series of ad hoc bilateral agreements. He offers the analogy of a "hub-and-spoke" model in which the United States negotiates separate bilateral agreements with its trading partners and argues that this is clearly an inferior prospect for smaller countries such as Canada and Mexico. Lipsey makes a strong argument for recognizing that increasing economic interdependence is a fact of modern life and that protectionist attitudes towards trade and investment are luxuries that countries can no longer afford.

While acknowledging the practical difficulty of negotiating and implementing a trilateral agreement, Lipsey provides a number of valuable suggestions by way of guidelines. He posits that an agreement should aim at the following objectives: (i) preserve the existing Canada-U.S. FTA intact; (ii) provide for a trilateral FTA that will give the three countries the access to each other's markets that they desire; (iii) settle specific issues (if any) between the U.S. and Mexico; and (iv) provide at least the core of an agreement to which other countries could accede.

The fifth chapter, prepared by Rosemary Piper and Alan Reynolds of the Hudson Institute, evaluates the relevance of the European Common Market experience for North American economic integration. They authors show that many concerns expressed by opponents of a North American common market were also expressed in the European context, and that economic and political means were identified to allay these concerns. Moreover, the large economic gains associated with European economic integration are plausible for North America. Piper and Reynolds debunk concerns that economic integration implies a loss of political sovereignty, although they underscore the need for harmonization of fiscal and monetary policies. They also note that concerns about a loss of cultural sovereignty have proven, to date, to be highly exaggerated.

The final chapter is an appendix prepared by Professor Steven Globerman and Ms. Maureen Bader. It provides an overview of the current state of economic integration in North America. In particular, it highlights recent movements towards trade and investment liberalization in the North American context along with the major outstanding barriers to closer economic relations among Canada, Mexico, and the United States.

On the whole, this volume provides a broad set of arguments in favour of dismantling barriers to trade and investment on a North American basis. The authors acknowledge that further movements towards this liberalized regime will impose dislocations and risks upon broad groups in each of the countries; however, failure to acknowledge international business developments that are increasing the costs associated with a balkanized North American market will impose even greater long-run dislocations and risks.

International competition is a fact of life facing all sovereign countries. Rapid movement of capital and production facilities from high-cost to low-cost locations is another. Free trade is ultimately a means to improve the long-run efficiency of North America in an international context and therefore a means to promote higher real income levels in all three countries. Arguably, the economic co-operation underlying a dismantling of barriers to trade and investment will also promote co-operation in other areas such as environmental protection and the use of marine resources. In short, the increases in real income levels from economic integration should be seen as only one dimension of the overall gains that will derive from a co-operative approach toward the use of all of our natural and man-made resources.

Steven Globerman

About the Authors

Steven Globerman

Steven Globerman holds a Ph.D. in economics and is currently professor of economics at Simon Fraser University and Adjunct Scholar at the Fraser Institute. He has served on the Faculty of Commerce and Business Administration at the University of British Columbia, the Faculty of Administrative Studies at York University, and the Faculty of Business Administration at Simon Fraser University. He has consulted for government agencies and private sector organizations and has published over 50 journal articles and 15 books and monographs on various aspects of economics and public policy.

Maureen Bader is enrolled in the M.B.A. program at Simon Fraser University's Faculty of Business Administration. She obtained her undergraduate degree in Mexico.

Richard G. Lipsey

Dr. Lipsey, F.R.S.C., is currently professor of economics at Simon Fraser University and Alcan Fellow of the Canadian Institute for Advanced Research for whom he is directing a large-scale international research project on economic growth and policy. Dr. Lipsey received his B.A. from the University of British Columbia in 1951, M.A. from the University of Toronto in 1953, and Ph.D. from London School of Economics. He was chairman of the Department of Economics and dean of the Faculty of Social Science at the new University of Essex, England, from 1964 to 1970. From 1970 to 1986, he was Sir Edward Peacock professor of economics, Queen's University. From 1983 to 1989, he was senior economic advisor for the C.D. Howe Institute. Dr. Lipsey has authored several textbooks in economics and published over 80 articles on various aspects of theoretical and applied economics.

Rogelio Ramirez de la O

Rogelio Ramirez de la O holds a Ph.D. in economics from Cambridge University (Fitzwilliam College) and a B.A. in economics from the National Autonomous University of Mexico. His specialization and doctoral dissertation on foreign direct investment in Mexico was published in 1983 in a less technical form, entitled "From Improvisation to Failure—The Policy of Foreign Investment in Mexico." He has published numerous other works on international investment, foreign trade, and, in recent years, Mexican economic policy.

He is the sole partner and president of Ecanal, S.A. (Economic Analysis for Company Planning), a firm whose periodic analysis of the Mexican economy and government policy is directed at major corporate clients, including some of the largest multinational firms. Ecanal has been publishing the monthly *Economic Report on Mexico* and the quarterly *Special Report on Mexico* since it was founded in 1977 by the British economist, the late Dr. Rodvers Opie. Before joining Ecanal, Dr. Ramirez worked for two years at the United Nations Centre for Transnational Corporations in New York, where he researched the influence of transnational corporations on the balance of payments and on intra-firm international trade.

He is a member of the American Economic Association and the Royal Economic Society, advisor to top management of several multinational firms, and provost of the University of the Americas.

Rosemary P. Piper

Rosemary Piper is a research fellow at Hudson Institute in Indianapolis. Ms. Piper, who specializes in economic policy issues, works with Mr. Alan Reynolds on the North America Common Market project. She also works with Dr. Robert Costello on the project, "An American Agenda for Leadership in Manufacturing and Technology," focusing on trade issues and product liability reform.

Prior to joining Hudson, Ms. Piper was an associate in the Corporate Finance Division of the Chase Manhattan Bank. In this position, she completed detailed studies of companies in the pharmaceutical, defence electronics, energy, and services industries. Ms. Piper's earlier experience focused on debt and development issues. She worked as a financial analyst in the Brazilian division of the World Bank, as an associate with the debt-equity swap team at American Express Bank, and as a statistical analyst for a small enterprise loan program in Costa Rica.

Ms. Piper holds an A.B. in social studies from Harvard University and an M.B.A. in finance and international business from Columbia University. She is a member of the Beta Gamma Sigma honors society and was chosen as an International Fellow at Columbia.

Alan Reynolds

Alan Reynolds became director of Economic Research at Hudson Institute in May 1990. He was formerly chief economist with Polyconomics, Inc., a New Jersey research organization.

Mr. Reynolds is a regular contributor to *Forbes, The Wall Street Journal,* and *National Review,* and has also been published in numerous other journals, including *Fortune, Policy Review, The Cato Journal,* and *The Harvard Business Review.* He has appeared on such television programs as "Wall Street Week" and "The MacNeil-Lehrer Newshour." Previously one of a select group of "Blue Chip" forecasters, Reynolds received acclaim for the accuracy of his predictions from Barron's, *Bondweek,* and *The Wall Street Journal.*

Mr. Reynolds has served as vice president of The First National Bank of Chicago and as senior economist with Argus Research. He was a member of Ronald Reagan's Inflation Task Force in 1980 and subsequently served on the Transition Team at the Office of Management and Budget. His essays have appeared in books and other publications of Kenyon College, Georgetown University, the Reason Foundation, the Heritage Foundation, the Tax Foundation, the Pacific Institute, the Media Institute, the Conference Board, and the Federal Reserve Banks of St. Louis and Atlanta.

Mr. Reynolds received his B.A. in economics from the University of California at Los Angeles and did graduate work at Sacramento State College.

Clark W. Reynolds

Clark Reynolds has been a professor of economics at the Food Research Institute at Stanford University since 1967. In 1980 he became founding director of the Americas Program, an interdisciplinary program that sponsors research in the social, economic, and political aspects of development in the Americas, and in regional and international exchange. His particular research interests include trade, finance, employment, the political economy of development, and the structure and growth of developing countries. Professor Reynolds received his B.A. from Claremont Men's College and attended the Massachusetts Institute of Technology and the Harvard Divinity School before receiving his M.A. and Ph.D. in economics from the University of California at Berkeley. He has taught at Yale University and Occidental College, and has been a visiting scholar at the National University of Mexico, El Colegio de Mexico, the International Institute for Applied Systems Analysis in Austria, the Stockholm School of Economics, and the University of Stockholm's Latin American Institute. Professor Reynolds is the author of numerous publications, the most recent being *The Dynamics of North American Trade and Investment: Canada, Mexico, and the United States* (Stanford University Press, 1991), which he co-authored. In addition, he is writing a sequel to the 1970 volume, *The Mexican Economy: Twentieth Century Structure and Growth,* to be entitled *The Mexican Economy: Managing Interdependence.* With colleagues in Canada and Mexico, he co-ordinates the North American Project which considers the implications of interdependence for the three North American partners.

Leonard Waverman

Dr. Waverman is a professor in the Department of Economics, University of Toronto, and director of the University's Centre for International Studies. He received his B.Com. and M.A. from the University of Toronto (1964 and 1965, respectively) and his Ph.D. from M.I.T. in 1969. He has been a visiting scholar at the University of Essex, Stanford University, and the Sloan School at M.I.T. Dr. Waverman specializes in industrial organization, and anti-trust, energy, and telecommunications economics. He has authored numerous scholarly works, was a board member of the Ontario Energy Board, and currently is a board member of the Ontario Telephone Service Commission. He has consulted widely in both Canada and the U.S.

He is the editor of the *Energy Journal* and has been associate editor of the *Canadian Journal of Economics*. He has also served on the Executive Committee of the European Association for Research in Industrial Economics. In 1991 he will be a visiting professor at INSEAD in Fontainebleau, France.

Chapter 1

A Mexican Vision of North American Economic Integration

Rogelio Ramirez de la O[1]

Background

From the end of the 1970s, the industrialized countries entered a new cycle of economic policy and growth after more than a decade of dismal economic performance. In the U.S. and the U.K., in particular, economic woes included the longest period of inflation recorded in history during peace-time, the devaluation of the pound sterling, and the near destruction of the dollar as a reserve currency. World inflation was accompanied by wide fluctuations in output and employment, large fiscal deficits, and weak capital formation.

The two oil shocks in 1973 and 1979-80 exacerbated these problems, but at the end of the seventies, when the second shock came, the governments of industrialized countries were not willing to accommodate cost increases and ignore high inflation. A change of economic regime took place, most markedly in the U.K. and the U.S., where anti-inflation policies received top priority. Other countries followed similar policies since the early eighties.

The change of regime was based on a revised view in both governments and international economic institutions, such as the IMF, the World Bank, and the OECD, of the role of the state, and a reformulation of the public sector/private

1   I appreciate the assistance of Mr. Edgar Aragon in the collection and processing of the statistical data, and the comments and suggestions Steven Globerman of the Fraser Institute made to improve this paper, but all remaining errors are my own responsibility.

sector mix in the economy to acknowledge the need for a withdrawal of the state from economic activity. Taxes were reduced in many countries, welfare systems were reformed and in many instances trimmed down, state entities were privatized, and trade protectionism was attacked and in numerous instances reduced. The private sector recovered its position as the main engine of growth, as international trade increased and national markets became increasingly integrated into a global economy. The world lived one of its longest periods of steady economic growth, and export-oriented economies showed particularly good performance.

Latin America, unfortunately, did not benefit from this expansion in world economic activity, as it entered at the same time its longest period of economic stagnation since the Great Depression. Its economic expansion during the seventies was largely based on good luck rather than good economic fundamentals. World inflation at the beginning of the decade increased primary commodity prices, including oil, while a glut of financial savings accumulated by oil exporters gave rise to increasing bank credit from commercial institutions of which Latin America borrowed a large part. An economic crisis unfolded as soon as commodity prices fell and bank credit was interrupted.

Temporarily high commodity prices and the large foreign indebtedness allowed Latin American governments to maintain mistaken economic policies (state expansion, fiscal deficits, inflation) for a longer period than the industrialized countries. When the U.S. and European countries changed policies, Latin America faced a world recession, weakened external markets, and rising interest rates.

Mexico achieved high growth from 1978 through 1981 aided by oil prices and foreign lending. But its government's economic policy was wrong, as it led to increasing fiscal deficits and high inflation, which its policy-makers maintained was the price to pay for economic growth and employment. Such a conceptual error ultimately cost Mexico a full decade of growth and progress. GDP stagnated following the so-called "debt crisis": from 1982 through 1989 it rose by only 0.1 percent annually. By comparison, population grew by 13 million in the Census count, approximately 2.3 percent per annum, and probably would have shown a greater increase if increased illegal migration to the United States had been taken into account.

The economic crisis predictably gave rise to political pressures. Opposition to the one-party system, never particularly strong since the creation of the PRI, gained popular support, and the socio-political fabric began to come apart as labour felt the effects of nil economic growth and reductions in real wages. Discontent over economic conditions led the government to undertake painful economic reforms, in line with what had proven feasible in industrialized countries. Changes in economic policy in Mexico thus emulated changes in the world economy, although several years apart.

World Trade Blocks

There are three main blocks of countries in the world which represent the bulk of world trade and show signs of increasing integration: the Asia and Pacific region, the European Community, and North America.

Asia

Asia and the Pacific (A&P) realized international trade transactions in 1988 of $1,279 billion ($1.3 trillion), 23.0 percent and 20.5 percent of world exports and imports respectively. Their exports grew annually at 15.2 percent in current dollars between 1973 and 1988, of which 42.5 percent in 1988 was intraregional trade. Exports within the region grew at a slower rate than total exports, For example, from 1980 to 1987, these annual rates were 7.5 percent and 8.5 percent respectively, the latter owing to especially high exports to North America which increased by a staggering 16.9 percent annually during the 15 years through 1988. This compares to a growth of 10.9 percent annually in exports from the rest of the world to North America.

The bulk of A&P exports is accounted for by Japan (39.5 percent of the total or $265 billion). Other large exporters are Hong Kong (9.5 percent), South Korea (9.0 percent), Taiwan (9.0 percent), China (7.0 percent), Singapore (6.0 percent), Australia (5.0 percent), Malaysia (3.0 percent), Indonesia (3.0 percent), and Thailand (2.5 percent). In 1988 these ten countries exported $626.5 billion and imported $537.8 billion, i.e., 143 percent and 94 percent of combined U.S. and Canadian exports and imports respectively, and 58.7 percent and 49.6 percent of European Economic Community (EC) exports and imports.

As table 1 shows, the A&P region, excluding China, has the largest population of the three world trade blocks mentioned above, with 499 million inhabitants, largely concentrated in Japan and Indonesia. It is followed by North America (the U.S., Canada, and Mexico) with 356 million, and the EC with 324 million. In terms of GDP per capita, the A&P region comes third after North America and Europe, but Japan, Australia, New Zealand, Hong Kong, and Singapore enjoy high per capita incomes.

The economic success of A&P countries, especially their rapid growth based on manufactured exports is viewed in Mexico with great interest, as are Japan's and South Korea's mastering of increasingly complex industrial processes, and the high level of co-ordination between governments and private conglomerates.

Nevertheless, not enough attention has been paid in Mexico to the fact that the rapid economic expansion in North America was crucial for the export

Table 1
Basic Indicators of Trading Blocks

Area/Country	Population (millions)	Area (Thousand km2)	GDP (millions USD 1988)	GDP 1980-88 (annual average)	GDP per capita (USD 1988)	Trade (millions USD 1988) Exports	Imports	Inflation (Average rate 1980-88)
North America	**356.0**	**21307**	**5459870**			**447335**	**589765**	
United States	246.3	9373	4847310	3.3	19840	315313	458682	4.0
Canada	26.0	9976	435860	3.3	16960	111364	112180	4.6
Mexico	83.7	1958	176700	0.5	1760	20658	18903	73.8
Pacific Area	**498.8**	**11483**	**3584540**			**585689**	**482279**	
Japan	122.6	378	2843710	3.9	21020	264772	183252	1.3
Taiwan						60382	44584	
South Korea	42.0	99	171310	9.9	3600	60696	51811	5.0
Hong Kong	5.7	1	44830	7.3	9220	63161	63894	6.7
New Zealand	3.3	269	39800	2.2	10000	8785	7304	11.4
Australia	16.5	7687	245950	3.3	12340	25283	29318	7.8
Singapore	2.6	1	23880	5.7	9070	39205	43765	1.2
Indonesia	174.8	1905	83220	5.1	440	19677	15732	8.5
Malaysia	16.9	330	34680	4.6	1940	20848	16584	1.3
Thailand	54.5	513	57950	6.0	1000	15806	17876	3.1
Philippines	59.9	300	39210	0.1	630	7074	8159	15.6

(continued on next page)

Table 1 (continued)

Area/Country	Population (millions)	Area (Thousand km2)	GDP (millions USD 1988)	GDP 1980-88 (annual average)	GDP per capita (USD 1988)	Trade (millions USD 1988)		Inflation (Average rate 1980-88)
						Exports	Imports	
European Community	**324.3**	**2257**	**4606840**			**1052854**	**1072031**	
Spain	39.0	505	340320	2.5	7740	40458	60434	10.1
Ireland	3.5	70	27820	1.7	7750	18736	15558	8.0
United Kingdom	57.1	245	702370	2.8	12810	145076	189466	5.7
Italy	57.4	301	828850	2.2	13330	128534	135514	11.0
Belgium	9.9	31	153810	1.4	14490	88953	91098	4.8
Netherlands	14.8	37	228280	1.6	14520	103206	99743	2.0
France	55.9	552	949440	1.8	16090	161702	176745	7.1
Denmark	5.1	43	90530	2.2	18450	27816	26458	6.3
Germany, Fed. Rep. of	61.3	249	1201820	1.8	18480	322555	248999	2.8
Portugal	10.3	92	41700	0.8	3650	10418	16038	20.1
Greece	10.0	132	40900	1.4	4800	5400	11978	18.9

Source: World Bank Development Report, 1990.

success of Asian countries. The high growth rates of Asian newly industrialized economies (Korea, Taiwan, Hong Kong, and Singapore) of 8.0 percent per annum in 1980-88 was substantively determined by their access to world markets, especially in the United States, although the good economic policies pursued in many of these countries should not be ignored. Other Asian countries (Indonesia, Malaysia, the Philippines, and Thailand) also recorded high growth rates in recent years, i.e., 5.3 percent and 7.4 percent on average in 1987 and 1988.

North America imported $187.7 billion from A&P in 1988, an annual increase in imports of 16.9 percent, as was mentioned earlier, and these countries represented 34.8 percent of North America's imports in 1988, compared to 19.6 percent in 1973. In fact, A&P exports penetrated North American markets at a much higher rate than Western European or Latin American exports: EC exports to North America grew by 11.5 percent annually during the period 1973-88, compared with growth in its total exports of 11.2 percent, while Latin American exports to North America grew annually by 11.2 percent compared with 9.9 percent for its total exports. Even intraregional North American trade (Canada-U.S.) increased less than Asian exports: 10.5 percent annually in the period 1973-88.

The penetration of A&P exports to Western Europe is equally impressive, with an annual growth rate of 15.7 percent in 1973-89, compared with European export growth of 10.9 percent. There is no doubt, therefore, that A&P have mastered production of manufactures with high demand elasticities in the industrialized world as well as trade strategies to conquer their markets.

Western Europe

Table 1 shows the European Economic Community as the second largest of the three regional trade blocks considered. The recent rate of growth of these countries is not as high as that of A&P countries, but its level of per capita income is much higher. The value of its foreign trade is larger than that of A&P and North America. In 1988 the EC exported $1,083 billion, or 135 percent more than North America and Mexico and 80 percent more than A&P.

Nevertheless, European exports, by contrast to A&P exports, are concentrated in the same region; i.e., 71.3 percent of exports are directed at Western Europe itself. The European Community is responsible for $1,065 million (still higher than North America and A&P), and 50 percent are intra-EC exports. Western European exports to North America are only 8.9 percent of its total exports and grew at an 11.5 percent annual rate during 1973-89, while its imports from North America are no more than 7.8 percent of its total imports, and grew by only 9.5 percent annually in 1973-89. Western European trade does not show the large regional imbalances as North America's or A&P's,

except in the case of Japan, with which Europe runs a large deficit (-$31 billion in 1988).

Europe has the most advanced form of regional economic co-operation. Its cultural homogeneity, similar levels of per capita income in the member countries, and physical proximity are unique to that region. Joint enterprises based on multinational resources, such as Airbus or the Channel Tunnel, cannot be copied elsewhere, unless there is an advanced form of economic integration.

Nevertheless, the European model establishes some valuable examples for Mexico. One is the European Monetary System, which has allowed the smaller economies to reduce inflation at home while pegging their currencies to the European Currency Unit (ECU), itself influenced by the strength of the deutsche mark. Inflation-prone countries such as Italy or Spain have gained from this association, and are likely to gain more in the future from further European integration.

Traditionally, Mexico has had an important trade relationship with Europe. Its trade with Spain, France, and Germany surpasses its trade with Canada, as table 2 shows. But perhaps more important than trade are European investments, particularly those from the U.K. and Germany, which have a long history in Mexico. Recent changes in Eastern Europe nevertheless reduce the potential for Western European investment in Mexico, not only because it will consume scarce resources but also because it will contribute to raising the cost of capital world-wide and will occupy the time of top European management to a degree that investments in other parts of the world receive only secondary priority. This situation has forced the Mexican government and private sector to reappraise our own regional interests. Not surprisingly, this led to the generalised view that an FTA with the U.S. and Canada could put Mexico again in a position to capture large amounts of foreign investment, mainly from North America.

North America

The United States and Canada are viewed in Mexico as two countries with very similar economic and cultural characteristics. The two economies have prevalent Anglo-Saxon roots, are rich in natural resources and in levels of per capita income, have very similar consumer patterns, and share a long border of 6,415 kilometres excluding the border between Canada and the state of Alaska.

Their economic exchanges are much larger than those between the U.S. and Mexico. For example, United States investment in Canada in 1988 was $4.1 billion, compared with $0.6 billion in Mexico. The estimated stock of U.S. investment in Canada is $61.2 billion, compared with that reported by the U.S. Department of Commerce for Mexico of $5.5 billion. Thus, apart from the particular interest that Mexico may represent for the United States, the level of economic exchanges between the U.S. and Canada suggests that their trade

Table 2
Mexico's International Trade
($ Million)

	1988		1989	
	Exports	Imports	Exports	Imports
Total	20,565	18,898	22,765	23,410
Canada	277	338	228	421
U.S.	13,533	12,612	15,787	15,862
Central America, ALADI	1,171	607	1,180	758
Caribbean and others	533	147	631	231
EEC	2,690	2,783	2,665	3,396
Japan	1,231		1,315	1,081
Memorandum:				
Brazil	116	296	193	361
Cuba	119	7	109	14
Argentina	125	135	113	137
Guatemala	109	30	158	32
Spain	981	208	1,134	329
France	562	437	482	565
Germany, Fed. Rep. of	440	1,187	363	1,370
China	180	105	94	196

Source: Banco Nacional de Comercio Exterior, Comercio Exterior, Vol. 40, No. 7, Julio 1990.

relations and economic integration are more advanced than anything Mexico can pursue with the United States on a bilateral basis. This fact is not well understood in Mexico, perhaps because of the large share that Mexico-U.S. transactions represent for Mexico's international economic exposure. The latter makes Mexico's trade and investment flows with other countries look relatively unimportant. Conversely, a U.S.-Mexico free trade agreement will probably not be a prominent economic issue in the United States except among specialized trade and political circles.

U.S. exports to Canada were $69.2 billion in 1988, compared with those destined for Mexico of $21 billion. U.S. imports from Canada were $81.4 billion, also higher than those from Mexico of $24 billion. Canada is the U.S.'s first client and its second supplier. Mexico is its third client and its fifth supplier.

The Free Trade Agreement between the United States and Canada, in force since 1989, awoke Mexico to the reality that trade blocks can cause some trade diversion, and at the present international juncture they are becoming acceptable means to accelerate economic integration between countries. Moreover, with the Latin American economies still in economic crisis, there has been a perceived risk in Mexico that the country will remain isolated from trade blocks, with the latter being mechanisms for economic growth in the 1990s. To stay outside these blocks would expose Mexico not only to the negative effects of trade diversion but also to the potential loss of direct investment which would take place if the country did become part of an enlarged market.

Mexico also recently awoke to the importance of foreign direct investment (FDI) as a mechanism for increasing the rate of economic growth and for participating in international trade flows. The importance of FDI is even greater today, since the current account deficit on Mexico's balance of payments has widened systematically since 1988, partly associated with Mexico's economic recovery and the peso appreciation that has accompanied anti-inflation policies. Thus, FDI now plays a role in financing the current deficit, and also in enhancing the confidence of the markets in the soundness of Mexico's macro-economic program. It is rightly seen in Mexico that FDI would be encouraged by greater economic integration with North America, beginning with an FTA.

Latin America

The phrase "the lost decade," coined in Latin America to describe the economic stagnation of the 1980s, captures the present mood of this region. Following the debt crisis, the region witnessed the vanishing of foreign credit, falling commodity prices, inflation, capital flight, and a general economic decline.

During the eighties, Latin America recorded economic growth of 1.6 percent annually, with large falls suffered in Mexico and Venezuela, inflation and financial crisis in Argentina and Brazil, stagnation in the smaller countries, and a mild economic recovery in Chile. Colombia, with a diversified economy and without the fiscal crisis and excessive foreign indebtedness that affected other large countries, performed better during the eighties, but its growth potential was undoubtedly diminished by the bad conditions in the surrounding nations.

Political unrest, military interventions, abrupt changes in economic legislation, and fiscal crises caused Latin America's trade and investment position in the world to decline over the last three decades. These developments scared foreign investment away. While in 1970, Latin America absorbed 13.9 percent of U.S. direct investment abroad, in 1989 it absorbed only 10.4 percent.

Latin America exported $122 billion in 1988 and recorded export growth of 9.9 percent annually during 1973-88. Its imports were $116.1 billion and grew at a 9.2 percent annual rate over the period 1973-88. By contrast to Europe, intraregional trade represented only $16.4 billion or 13.4 percent of total trade in 1988, a reflection of weak domestic markets. Mexico, in particular, has always found its main trading partner outside the region: today the United States; England during most of the nineteenth century until the late 1870s.

Successive Mexican governments have tried to induce a geographical diversification of trade away from the United States, partly as a nationalistic attitude to emphasize economic and political independence. Attempts at Latin American integration in the sixties and multilateral agreements to reduce trade tariffs for goods from the region under ALALC (Latin American Free Trade Association), and later on under ALADI (Latin American Integration Association), did not cause a change in the regional structure of Mexico's trade, for only 6 percent of its exports and 3 percent of its imports are with the region.

Several factors explain this. Firstly, despite granting trade preferences, Latin American economies remain largely closed to free trade, and quantitative import restrictions remain in various countries. Secondly, a wave of economic nationalism in the early seventies led to the introduction of restrictions on foreign investment, which discouraged transnational enterprises outside the region from playing a potentially catalytic role to enhance trade linkages. Thirdly, significant barriers to physical communications and poor infrastructure make trade difficult, especially between Mexico and South America. Lastly, economic stagnation and poor economic policies have impeded growth and therefore trade.

Mexico now views Latin America as an area of opportunity for increased trade, even though this promise has not been realized in the past. While the potential exists, the consolidation of a strong Latin American block is probably a relatively distant possibility, although the initiative of the United States to strengthen regional ties could help accelerate this process if it is implemented.

Mexico, however, cannot base its short- and medium-term commercial policy on this possibility and must therefore reorient its interest toward North America.

Mexico's Economy in the 1980s

After the debt crisis hit Mexico and obliged it to suspend payments on its foreign debt and seek a loan from the IMF Extended Credit Facility, the domestic economy underwent a painful macro-economic restructuring based on dramatic fiscal and exchange rate adjustments. The combination of these two policies caused a deep contraction of the domestic market, which led Mexican industry to seek markets abroad.

The Mexican private sector, which was exceedingly indebted in dollars in 1982, received government support to restructure these obligations and thus avoided massive bankruptcy. A dramatic exchange-rate devaluation, which altered the relative prices of tradable and non-tradable goods in favour of one sector of the domestic manufacturing industry, and domestic price liberalization allowed firms to be profitable, even though their levels of capacity utilization were relatively low during most of the decade. Dramatic adjustments in relative prices thus set the stage for the gradual removal of trade restrictions.

Increased international trade had positive effects on domestic activity; nevertheless, the economy remained in recession throughout most of the eighties, given the small relative size of Mexico's export industries, the only industries to record any growth. Starting in 1983, Mexican industry began to experience dramatic increases in exports of manufactures, which recorded 22.6 percent annual growth over the period 1982-89. Manufactured exports became even more relevant as oil prices fell in 1985 and 1986, causing reductions in foreign-exchange earnings equivalent to 6.0 percent of GDP and a 38 percent devaluation of the real exchange rate of the peso. The share of oil in total exports thus fell from 78.4 percent in 1982 to 34.5 percent in 1989, while that of manufactures rose from 14.2 percent ($3.0 billion) to 55.0 percent ($12.5 billion) over the same period.

By the mid-eighties the Mexican government had realized that maintaining the engine of export growth required greater efficiency in manufacturing industries, which implied that it needed access to competitively priced materials. This led first to the creation of more facilities to effect temporary (in-bond) imports of raw materials. Later on, import licences and official prices, the main instruments of trade protection since the forties, were gradually removed. Trade liberalization took place in three stages. The first, from 1983 through 1985, involved the gradual reduction of protection, and in particular of import licenses. In 1982 all items in the import tariff were subject to prior license. By 1985 this applied to only 10 percent of the tariff items; i.e., 839 items out of a total of 8,091. The second stage in 1985 involved a "shock" reduction in tariffs, followed in 1986 by Mexico becoming a GATT member. The third stage, in December 1988, consisted of eliminating licences for many consumer goods accompanied by further tariff reductions to a maximum of 20 percent. It is plain to see through the experience of the 1980s that it was export industries that represented the strongest source of pressure to liberalize trade.

Owing to the close linkage between industrial regulations and trade, the Mexican government had to begin scrapping sectoral development plans. Some were elaborated in the seventies or even before, while others had been elaborated as recently as 1984, such as plans for a new pharmaceutical industry and an updated automotive industry. All such plans invariably included domestic-content requirements which prevented Mexican industry from maximizing exports. The changes were beneficial not only to exporters but also to Mexican industry in general, as it was forced to improve its competitive position. The automotive and computer industries were relieved of specific domestic-content requirements, and Mexico moved closer to the U.S. position on the issue of patents and trademark protection. In 1989 regulations on foreign direct investment were issued which made it possible to contemplate for the first time since 1973 majority foreign investment without specific legal exemptions. Such regulations are still far from a fully liberal regime, but this was regarded as a first step of a liberalizing policy which must continue in the 1990s.

The developments in Mexico's economy since 1982 can be summarized as consistent trade liberalization combined with macro-economic policies focused on curbing inflation against a background of nearly zero growth. Inflation remained high, always above 50 percent annually, and reached a peak of 159 percent in December 1987, when the government embarked on a price and wage control program, the Pact of Economic Solidarity. Part of the reason for the continued implementation of these policies in the midst of weak economic conditions was the economic and political support received by Mexico from Washington, which led to IMF and World Bank loans and, in 1989, to the renegotiation of Mexico's foreign debt with commercial banks.

Investment fell by an average of 3.3 percent annually from 1982 to 1988, which suggests that the country's capital stock decreased dramatically during the crisis years. Insufficient infrastructure and industrial capacity now represent the main constraint on future economic growth as economic recovery starts.

As Mexico enters the 1990s, the economy is on a healthier macro-economic footing. Public finances have been adjusted, the export structure is more diversified, and inflation has fallen from 3 to 2-digit levels. Moreover, the government gained the confidence of the private sector, even though removing trade and industrial protection hurt many privileged interests. Of course, more needs to be done in order to reduce inflation from the present 30 percent to 5 percent or even less, which is its level in the U.S. and Canada.

The move towards a free trade agreement with Canada and (especially) the United States is therefore a logical next step in the consolidation of trade and investment liberalization. It is needed to put future industrial and export growth on a stable footing in a global framework and to cement all recent economic reforms. Business confidence and foreign investment would be enhanced if such changes were incorporated into a formal framework which would be difficult to reverse in the future.

Reasons to Pursue Closer Economic Integration with North America

As a consequence of the 1980s economic crisis, Mexico chose to make economic changes that were much more dramatic than they appear from simple observation, or even from the analysis of economic data. These changes consisted of a revision of the old model of protected markets and heavy state intervention.

A lesson learned from these changes is that once implemented, they release new economic forces which then call for further changes. Until now, the most important change has been in the trade regime, which has far-reaching implications owing to the role of trade as a creator of changes in the pattern of demand and in the allocation of resources. The large industrial groups in Mexico that had to adjust their operations to a more liberal trade regime eventually demanded that the Mexican government provide greater macro-economic stability and less industrial regulation. Small companies, similarly, have faced increased competition from imports, which has obliged them to adjust operations, often reducing the number of products they manufacture in order to lengthen production runs for other products. The adjustment has not been easy; in many instances companies had to reduce output and in many others employment losses followed reduced sales. Small business demand for less government regulation has been even greater than that of large companies, as the former cannot otherwise adapt to the new circumstances with rigid labour or industrial regulations.

The government was therefore set on a pace of rapid changes in the scope of its regulations and in the institutions that make and apply the regulations. At the same time, it had to send consistent messages to the markets and make its new macro-economic policy convincing in order to fight inflation effectively. Only gradually has the new message been internalized by economic agents, and the transition between the old and a new regime has been a long one.

It is fair to say, however, that although the changes continue to take place today and will continue to impose significant costs of adjustment on domestic industry and employment, a substantial part of the costs of transforming a closed economy into an open economy has already occurred. Moreover, the long-run costs of returning to a protectionist stance would likely exceed any additional costs of adjusting to free trade.

Following this line of reasoning, closer formal economic ties with North America must be the next step to maximize gains from trade liberalization. Closer integration with North America is justified by the following factors:

- The integration would give domestic economic agents greater certainty that the trade and regulatory changes discussed here will be definitive. This would spark new investment by firms that are still uncertain about how soon they will face intensified competition or new export opportunities.

- The economic adjustment of industrial firms would be facilitated if the size of their potential markets was increased by economic integration, as they would find it more feasible to specialize in narrower ranges of products and continue to expand operations. While the need to specialize would result from liberalizing the trade regime anyway, access to a larger market would not be ensured in the absence of an FTA and associated closer economic integration.

- Economic integration of an informal and incomplete character with the United States already exists in the northern border cities of Mexico, which contributed to rapid progress in that region during the 1980s, even though the Mexican economy remained in recession. An FTA and greater formalized integration would widen the scope of this informal integration and transmit its effects to the rest of the country.

- As most Mexican labour migration is to the United States, the integration with North America could contribute to diminishing this flow by creating jobs in Mexico, thereby retaining potentially productive labour in Mexico.

- By the same token, integration would raise average wage rates in Mexico and therefore contribute to a better distribution of income.

- Finally, North America is a natural market for Mexico apart from being its main supplier of technologically advanced goods. An integration with these countries would enhance the technological standing of Mexican industry and would put Mexico on a path of continuous technical progress by facilitating access to sources of foreign technology.

Estimation of Economic Effects

Estimation of the effects of economic integration confront data and methodological limitations. Data are seldom available in a form required by the researcher to estimate effects. For example, such data as the size of the labour force in the export and import competing industries or average productivity in different sectors over time are extremely rare. Methodological limitations are even worse. The analysis of effects must cover all possible areas and interactions between sectors, but this is only possible with general equilibrium models which must be built ad hoc. Even so, the answers given by such models to the question of how much integration will affect output, trade, and employment must be taken as mere indications of the direction of change. This is because trade liberalization creates new economic forces which change the way in which the economy responds to the initial effect of increasing trade. Such forces in fact contribute to changing the economic structure on which the effects of trade were initially modelled and estimated. Ignoring these dynamic effects is one of the main reasons for the systematic underestimation of trade liberalization effects by econometric models.

We need not be concerned here with problems of estimation. Suffice to say that good models predict correctly the direction of the effect, i.e., whether trade and productivity levels are correlated and whether increasing exports contribute to higher income levels. In what follows I discuss the nature of the economic effects of an FTA that liberalizes trade.

Nature of Effects

There are two types of effects. Direct effects arise from the increase in exports and imports caused by the reduction of tariffs and the elimination of non-tariff barriers. The size of these effects depends upon how high the tariff and non-tariff barriers were before their elimination. Indirect effects, more interesting in an analytical sense, consist of changes that take place in economic variables, other than exports and imports, which would not have taken place in the absence of trade liberalization. Those variables include investment and output.

From econometric estimates reported in this chapter's appendix, we know that growth in Mexico's GDP is positively associated with increases in gross fixed investment (GFI). Also, the increase in output explains the largest part of the increase in imports. Imports and non-oil exports are also positively associated, such that the growth in the latter cannot be explained in the absence of growing imports. This means that additional investment must be made to sustain increasing exports and growth in output. My analysis, based on observations covering the period from January 1983 to December 1989, unfortunately cannot distinguish the direct from the indirect effects, but it does capture the direction of the initial effects of trade liberalization since 1985.

The relevant indirect effects of trade liberalization are, initially, an increase in imports associated with new investment and greater specialization, as trade liberalization makes foreign equipment and materials available to firms. Since these materials do not have to be produced locally, firms can specialize in narrower ranges of products and therefore produce more efficiently, which gives them the opportunity to serve foreign markets. Increased exports contribute to higher levels of output and higher rates of investment as more capacity is added. The new investment, in turn, calls for higher imports of capital goods. The initial increase in imports is thus associated with increasing exports and greater productivity, but this is not necessarily a visible effect. Of course, part of the increase in imports displaces domestic production of similar materials and equipment, and this may lead to output losses in other sectors different from those where exports begin to increase. This offsets part of the gain in output in export industries, but as long as it represents production which would not have been able to compete successfully against imports, its loss was inevitable under the gradual tariff reductions agreed to in GATT.

The reduction and removal of tariffs in foreign countries represent an additional push on exports, as the price advantage enjoyed by local producers is reduced. In addition, if the foreign country removes non-tariff barriers, exports can increase further as uncertainty over the future access to that market is removed. This facilitates domestic investment in plant and equipment.

Both the direct and indirect effects take place simultaneously. Domestic industry, for example, can experience a boost to output from reduced foreign tariffs, and exports can increase immediately if there is enough capacity available. At the same time, producers may begin to invest in additional plant and equipment in order to serve the foreign market now enhanced by the reduction of tariff and non-tariff barriers. The effects would be an increase in exports simultaneously with an increase in investment. Consequent with the latter, imports of capital goods begin to rise.

The increase in imports associated with the need for greater efficiency will be reinforced later on by the increase in imports associated with higher national income brought about by investment and exports.

A Crude Measurement of Macro-economic Effects

In what follows I attempt to estimate the short-run effects that are most likely to be felt in the economy following the FTA. These effects do not necessarily wait for signing the FTA, but, on the contrary, may largely precede the agreement, since producers will position themselves in anticipation of greater competition caused by foreign producers entering domestic markets, as well as to take advantage of new export opportunities. Some of the effects I discuss below are based on assumptions that seem to be reasonable, and they are intended only to illustrate the possible direction and size of effects. The following effects are considered over a hypothetical period of five years which I call the period of FTA implementation. The figures for the projection shown are those of base year 1990:

• Trade diversion effect, i.e., Mexican exports begin to displace exports of third countries to North America by virtue of the tariff reduction and the removal of non-tariff barriers, which grant Mexican exporters an advantage. For simplification, this effect is assumed to represent 5 percent of present U.S. imports from the rest of Latin America and some Asian countries (excluding Japan). The full trade-diversion effect is assumed to take place over a five-year period and represents an increase in Mexican non-oil exports of $1 billion annually (6.5 percent of exports today).

• A foreign market-growth effect on trade is obtained from assuming the same relationship between GDP growth and Mexican exports and imports as that observed during the period from 1985 to 1990. It must be noted that the parameters of the equation of Mexican exports estimated with monthly data from 1983 to 1989 and shown in the appendix are substantially higher than those estimated in time series which include much longer periods than I have considered (see Clavijo and Faini, 1990). The large difference must be attributed to the fact that in the period considered here U.S. imports expanded very rapidly while Mexico undertook a rapid liberalization of import trade, both of which should be reflected in a rapid expansion of trade in both directions. The parameters of our equations therefore reflect the initial effects of liberalized imports, an initial export boost facilitated by such liberalization and also by a profound depression in Mexico's domestic market. The parameters in the appendix, which I use to simulate imports and exports over the five-year implementation period of the FTA, therefore contain a large cyclical component. This means that it is probable that the rate of increase in Mexican imports in response to GDP growth, and in Mexican exports in response to U.S. and Canadian growth, will gradually decline once it reaches a maximum.

• A third effect of the FTA on Mexico is caused by the increase in GFI above its trend line, which would be associated with the increase in export opportunities and the upgrading in plant and equipment by firms that export or compete against imports. The increase in investment causes imports of capital goods to rise and also lifts the GDP trend line. The increase is in Mexico's total imports and not just those from North America, despite the fact that the latter enjoys a tariff advantage. Hence the rest of the world also benefits from the higher level of Mexican imports. It is difficult to say how much gross fixed investment should rise in order to sustain a steady growth in non-oil exports. During 1981 to 1989, it fell by 1.6 percent annually on average, owing to the abrupt falls in 1982 and 1986, while GDP rose by 1.4 percent annually. During the 1970s, GFI rose annually by 8.6 percent, recording jumps of double this average at the end of the decade, while GDP rose by 6.6 percent annually. In more recent years (1985 to 1989), since trade liberalization started, GFI rose 1.5 percent annually while GDP rose by 0.96 percent. Given that much of the public infrastructure and basic industries has been neglected during the long period of weak investment, it seems likely that the rates of increase of GFI will be much higher than historical trends suggest in order to sustain a steady export drive. It seems unlikely, however, that sufficient resources will be available to Mexico to sustain very high rates of investment. I have assumed that investment increases in order to reduce the differential in output per worker between North America and Mexico from 5 to 1 at present to 3.7 to 1 five years after the FTA begins. With unchanged capital/output ratios, output per worker rises in Mexico by 6.5 percent annually compared with 2.0 percent arbitrarily assumed for North America. Investment must increase, in addition, in order to maintain a 2.0 percent steady annual increase in employment. The resulting increase in GFI is 8.2 percent annually.

- A fourth effect of the FTA is on trade of non-factor services, since these are usually associated to a large degree with sales of goods. These services include transport, insurance, distribution, and communications. The same parameters employed in the estimation of exports and imports of goods are used for non-factor services.

- Initially, no increase in oil exports is projected as a consequence of the FTA. The volume of oil exports is assumed to continue at approximately 1.4 millions of barrels per day (MBD), while prices are assumed to increase to $26.50 per barrel in the first year of the implementation and to fall to $23.50 per barrel in the second year. The price assumed for the rest of the period is $23.50. Price assumptions reflect extensive damage to Middle East capacity caused by the war in the Persian Gulf. But even with such prices, the trade deficit grows rapidly, and increases in the volume of exports appear to be necessary from the third year onwards to reach 2.6 MBD by the fifth year. The reason for assuming an increase in volume of exports is the rapid deterioration observed in the non-oil trade account which I discuss later. The increase in oil trade is not a direct consequence of the FTA but rather results from increased trade and the need to increase either direct or portfolio investment. Since the oil sector looms so large in Mexico, it does not seem feasible that massive in-flows of foreign investment into Mexico can take place without reducing restrictions on private investment in oil.

- The projected values of imports and exports of goods and services are complemented by some conventional estimates of factor service payments which allows me to reach a crude estimate of the current account of the balance of payments over the relevant period.

- An adjustment effect is assumed in order to compare the gains from increased integration with the losses to Mexican industry associated with displaced sales by increased imports. Needless to say, this is a crude estimate based on the assumption that one-third of Mexican manufacturing will not record any growth over the implementation period. The cost of adjustment would be the rate of growth for the whole manufacturing industry recorded in the absence of the FTA, an estimated 4.0 percent annually, multiplied by the size of this one-third of industry over the relevant period. This assumption is not entirely arbitrary: manufacturing output rose by 7.5 percent annually from 1977 to 1981 and by 0.9 percent annually from 1982 to 1989, with effects of trade liberalization already present in the latter period, but also with a deep recession in domestic markets. It is assumed then that with moderate economic growth, manufacturing could probably grow by 4.0 percent annually in the absence of an FTA with North America, which is well above the rate experienced in the 1980s, but lower than the rate of the late 1970s. The ratio of one-third is obtained from the share of industries that were badly hit during the 1982-89 period in terms of total output of the industry. These industries are not likely to recover with a free trade agreement. But by the same token, industries that survived the opening of trade and the recession in domestic markets should not, on the whole, be doing much worse in the 1990s.

Probable Effects of an FTA

The estimation, as shown in table 3, suggests that GDP annual growth would rise to between 4.1 percent and 4.9 percent annually, i.e., 1.2 percentage points above the 3.5 percent rate considered feasible at present: in 1989 growth was 2.8 percent and in 1990 it is expected to be about 3.2 percent. This is a 17.0 percent increased sustained rate of growth accompanied by a rapid growth in non-oil exports from $18.4 billion in year one of the FTA to $34.0 billion in year five; i.e., a 13.7 percent sustained rate of growth, not very different from that observed in the five years to 1989 (14.6 percent in current dollars). It should be noted that part of the export growth of the last five years was based on weak domestic markets and excess capacity in large segments of Mexican industry.

Table 3
North American Free Trade Area Effects on Mexico's Economy
Period of Implementation Year 1 to Year 5

Years	1989	1990	1	2	3	4	5
External Variables							
a) Real exchange rate %	1.07	1	0.995	0.99	0.986	0.981	0.976
b) GDP U.S. growth %	2.8	2.5	2.5	2.5	2.5	2.5	2.5
c) Trade diversion $Blln	0	0	1	1	1	1	1
d) Volume oil export MBD	1.236	1.236	1.4	1.5	1.9	2.1	2.6
e) Oil export price $PB	15.1	19	18	18	18	18	18
f) Factor service $Blln	7.6	6.6	6.5	6.5	6.5	6.5	6.5
g) Capital repatriation $Blln	2.5	3	4	5	5	4	3
h) Foreign direct investment $Blln	2.2	3	4	5	5	5	5
i) Adjustment cost GDP%	0	0	0.5	0.5	0.5	0.5	0.5
j) Investment growth %	6.6	10.8	8.2	8.2	8.2	8.2	8.2
Effects							
a) GDP Mexico growth %	3.1	3.0	4.1	4.6	4.8	4.9	4.9
b) Manufactures output %	7.1	7.0	4.6	5.5	5.6	5.5	5.5

(continued on next page)

Table 3 (continued)

Years	1989	1990	1	2	3	4	5
c) Non-oil exports $Blln	14.9	15.5	18.4	21.7	25.3	29.4	34.0
d) Oil exports $Blln	7.9	10	9.2	9.9	12.5	13.8	17.1
e) Imports $Blln	23.4	27.0	31.9	38.4	46.6	56.6	68.8
f) Labour employment %	3.0	2.7	1.8	2.0	2.0	2.0	1.9
g) Labour productivity %	3.0	3.0	3.0	3.2	3.2	3.2	3.2
h) Capital productivity %	3.0	3.0	3.3	3.1	3.0	2.9	2.8
i) Trade Balance $Blln	-0.6	-1.5	-4.3	-6.9	-8.8	-13.4	-17.7
j) GDP Mexico $Blln	201.0	227.0	236.4	247.3	259.3	272.0	285.3
k) Exports/GDP	11.3	10.6	11.7	12.7	14.6	15.9	17.9
l) Imports/GDP	11.6	11.9	13.5	15.5	18.0	20.8	24.1
m) Export services $Blln	10.8	11.3	12.7	14.2	16.0	18.0	20.1
n) Import services $Blln	8.0	9.1	10.8	12.9	15.7	19.1	23.2
o) Curr. acc. exc. debt serv. $Blln	2.2	0.7	-2.4	-5.6	-8.5	-14.5	-20.7
p) Curr. account $Blln	-5.4	-5.9	-8.9	-12.1	-15.0	-21.0	-27.2
q) Curr. acc. exc. debt/GDP	1.1	0.3	-1.0	-2.3	-3.3	-5.3	-7.3
r) Curr. account/GDP	-2.7	-2.6	-3.8	-4.9	-5.8	-7.7	-9.5
s) Foreign borr. requirem. $Blln	-0.7	0.1	-0.9	-2.1	-5.0	-12.0	-19.2

Source: Ecanal, January 31, 1991.

Nevertheless, the estimated growth rate is not unrealistic in the context of an FTA that encompasses a market 30 times the size of the Mexican market. Also, between one-fourth and one-third of the annual increase in projected non-oil exports could be trade diverted away from other countries. The increase in imports is spectacular at 20.6 percent annually, owing largely to the higher rate of investment and GDP growth, and also to the rapid increase in non-oil exports which are expected to consume increasing amounts of imported components and capital goods.

While high, the estimated increase in imports is not very different from that observed during 1984 to 1989 (15.9 percent annually). As noted earlier, the latter is largely explained by the liberalization of import trade in very rapid steps and, since 1988, also by the steady appreciation of the real exchange rate of the peso. Since a large part of the liberalization of imports has been already accomplished, and since the real peso exchange rate is not expected to appreciate significantly in coming years as inflation recedes in Mexico, it could be argued that import growth is not likely to be sustained at such high rates. Nevertheless, import growth in 1984 to 1989 took place with very low growth rates of GDP. Also, since domestic growth will absorb much of the still idle capacity in Mexican industry, a high rate of GDP growth can hardly take place without additional large increases in imports. It must be noted that import growth has been one of the most underestimated items in every government plan since trade liberalization began, with actual figures exceeding the government's by 11.5 percent in 1990 ($3.5 billion) and 13.0 percent ($2.7 billion) in 1989.

It has been suggested elsewhere (van Wijnbergen, 1990) that the rapid increase in imports observed in Mexico since 1987 is not caused by an investment boom. This seems to be corroborated by the low figures of investment growth. Van Wijnbergen's argument is that uncertainty over the possibility of a policy reversal, meaning a resumption of tariffs, leads to higher current imports than would be otherwise justified. Although this could imply that our high import elasticities grossly overestimate future import growth since an FTA would diminish uncertainty about a policy reversal, the high investment to support economic growth in a less uncertain environment must still be carried out. A reduction in import growth thus remains unlikely.

Policy Implications

The simulation suggests three specific policy implications. The first is that despite the rapid response of non-oil exports and increasing industrial efficiency, the current account deficit can be expected to widen over the period following the FTA. This makes it unlikely that oil exploration and production can be kept at their present levels. The need for massive investment in the oil sector is therefore self-evident, as oil represents a considerable part of Mexico's total exports. In other words, the expected growth in the domestic market could force Mexico to reduce oil exports unless a massive expansion in oil production is accomplished. An implication of an FTA agreement, because of the higher growth rates it brings about and the likelihood of higher non-oil current deficits, is that oil exports should not only be maintained but increased. The need for a substantial increase in oil industry extraction and refining capacity is therefore inescapable.

A second implication is that foreign direct investment and capital repatriation (which contains a portion of portfolio foreign investment) should contribute $8 to $10 billion annually to the financing of the current account. This implies substantially larger amounts than in recent years, although not unrealistic in the framework of an FTA. Nevertheless, encouraging this investment would require a much more deregulated regime in general and for various sectors in particular (including restricted industries) than exists today. It is hard to imagine foreign investment of such magnitude without a major opening of the energy and financial sectors to private investors.

A third implication is that the level of factor service payments, which includes interest on the foreign debt, will continue to represent a large portion of current transactions, even at a projected constant level over time. A further renegotiation of Mexico's foreign debt which reduces the burden of service payments, at least in the initial part of the FTA implementation, cannot be ruled out.

Even with the projected increase in foreign investment and capital repatriation, as well as an increase in oil exports, the current account deficit is expected to widen considerably over the projected period. This does not reflect the inefficiency of Mexican industry in the face of increased imports, but rather an increase in investment concomitant with an FTA that brings about increased growth and higher wages for Mexico. Despite this, the current account deficit on the balance of payments shown in table 3 could be too large in the fourth and fifth year of the FTA. The actual deficit could be smaller if import elasticities change over time once Mexican industry adjusts to a new mix of domestic/imported materials and inputs. Nevertheless, the projected deterioration suggests that macro-economic policy must be fine-tuned in order to avoid large imbalances once economic growth becomes steady. The experiences of Spain or the U.K. joining the EC during 1985 to 1990 indicate that it is only too common to generate large external imbalances once inflation recedes and investment and growth recover, and that avoiding a premature fiscal expansion, and maintaining low inflation and a strong exchange rate become essential for economic stability.

Some less specific macro-economic implications are worthy of brief mention. Mexico does not have controls on capital movements. With a widening current deficit and a large part of its financing in the form of short-term capital in-flows, the effectiveness of monetary policy in influencing domestic economic variables will be considerably diminished relative to that of fiscal policy. This will call for a more rigorous fiscal policy than we have observed for most of the 1980s. Such an implication is of even greater importance for a period of rapid investment growth, as fiscal policy aimed at keeping inflation under control may preclude large state investments in many development projects. The engine of future Mexican growth will therefore have to be the private sector, and this would undoubtedly require the continuation of economic and institutional reforms. The Government of Mexico must achieve a delicate political equilibrium in creating the consensus for these necessary changes, since many of them will imply, at least in the short run, the elimination of protection and privileges for sectors of the population. Hence it is important that the FTA be seen as a source of higher productivity and higher wage rates.

Mexican inflation must be reduced in the short run, since currency realignments would destroy confidence in financial markets. This is especially important as credibility for the government's policies is not yet firmly established. A real depreciation of the exchange rate would harm the capital in-flows projected to contribute to financing the current account deficit. Moreover, with monetary policy becoming less effective in the presence of such in-flows, there will be no alternative but to maintain a sound and austere fiscal policy. This sounds like a tall order for a developing economy with a rapid population growth rate and numerous social demands; nevertheless, trade integration with North America will make inflation in Mexico prohibitively costly.

Conclusions

International trade is bound to transform Mexico in unexpected ways, as it unleashes economic forces, exposes a myriad of untapped opportunities for entrepreneurial activity, and brings the forces of internationalization into the economy. Hence it is not an exaggeration to say that the signing of a free trade agreement with the United States and Canada will be the most important economic decision taken to date in Mexico, with implications for generations to come. An FTA will open the road toward greater economic integration in North America.

Mexico is likely to become the third country to integrate itself into the vast North American market and would be the only developing economy in a free trade area. This raises some difficult issues for economic policy, additional to those that must normally be addressed in the accession to a trade block, given the large differential in productivity and wage rates between Mexico and the

U.S. and Canada. Closing this differential will require that increases in Mexican exports be based on higher productivity, which calls for massive investment and imports. The resulting increase in trade should be spectacular, especially in Mexican imports essential for the increase in industrial capacity. Economic integration will therefore propel Mexico into a rush for capital.

Economic integration should be gradual, beginning first with an FTA between the three countries in the region, but then advancing into more complex forms of economic co-operation, ultimately including a North American common market. The signing of bilateral FTAs, therefore, between the U.S. and Canada, on the one hand, and the U.S. and Mexico, on the other, is less attractive than trilateral integration.

Economic integration should result in Mexican domestic markets growing at a much faster pace than those of its northern neighbours. Simple increases in Mexican exports based on low wages, which are often taken to be the logical course for a developing economy that becomes part of a trade block, should not form the basis of Mexico's economic strategy. By contrast, Mexico should seek comprehensive economic integration with North America, which would bring about the injection of foreign capital in order to sustain a steady growth based on higher productivity, higher wages, and larger domestic markets.

Such a strategy is admittedly more difficult to implement than simply encouraging exports of labour-intensive products, but it is nevertheless feasible, as has been illustrated by the successful integration of Spain into the EC. Success, however, requires that the policy agenda in Mexico be moved forward to carry out rapid economic reforms, of which two are essential. First are reforms to facilitate a smooth and efficient economic adjustment of domestic capital to trade liberalization. These comprise changes in the present legal and institutional framework for labour, industrial regulation, taxation, and the management of state-owned basic industries. Second are reforms enabling foreign capital to fully participate in the expansion of Mexican industry which should involve changes in the existing legislation affecting the energy and financial sectors. Only in this way would the need for additional resources resulting from the signing of an FTA with North America be met, and only then will the growth experienced in connection with increased trade benefit wage earners, as a larger stock of capital would raise output per worker on a sustained basis.

The signing of an FTA with the U.S. and Canada followed by more comprehensive economic integration will cause a profound transformation in Mexico's economic structure. The most important effects are not the visible, direct effects on trade volumes, which will increase as tariffs and non-tariff barriers are removed. Rather, the most important effects will be indirect, i.e., via changes in business and public attitudes which will eventually be reflected in economic decisions. The policy agenda for the next few years must include substantive economic and institutional reforms to accommodate these changes and the new investment sparked by them.

The economic integration of Mexico into North America is consistent with economic policy and reforms of recent years. These reforms were originally intended as a response to the economic crisis caused by previous bad economic policies, but they must now be put into the framework of a new economic policy regime which, among other things, will prevent the same mistakes from being committed in the future and will link Mexico to the dynamics of industrialized economies.

An FTA and continued economic integration will have effects that will be felt even before the relevant agreements are signed, as economic agents position themselves in anticipation of the change in regime. Direct effects, via the increase in Mexican exports and imports, and indirect effects via the increase in investment and economic growth induced by greater trade prospects should lift the rate of GDP growth in Mexico from 3.5 percent which is now considered feasible, to an average rate for the first five years of the FTA implementation of 4.7 percent.

The growth in activity will be largely based on a higher rate of investment, which is expected to grow 8.2 percent annually at a minimum. This rate assumes that the differential in output per worker between North America and Mexico is reduced from 5 to 1 to 3.7 to 1 within five years, i.e., an annual increase in output per worker of 6.5 percent combined with a 2.5 percent annual increase in employment of labour. A larger increase in employment would have to be combined with a lower increase in output per worker given the same growth in investment. The increase in output per worker will cause the most important indirect effects.

Imports are projected to increase by 20.6 percent per year, which, although not much higher than the increases of recent years, would be difficult to sustain without significant injections of foreign capital.. Non-oil exports are expected to increase at similarly high rates, aided not only by a high elasticity in the U.S. import demand, as the analysis of Mexican export performance suggests, but also by trade diversion away from other suppliers to the United States. Although annual export growth is projected at the high rate of 14.9 percent, it is below the rate of import growth for the basic reason that Mexico's economy is expected to grow at a much faster rate than the rest of North America.

The increase in Mexican imports of $41.8 billion between year one and year five represents additional purchases from North America of $24 to $35 billion by the fifth year of FTA implementation, assuming that the shares of the U.S. and Canada remain the same as today or increase slightly over time. Growth of the Mexican market would therefore boost North American exports to Mexico.

The latter could grow between 23 percent and 30 percent annually. Similarly, Mexican exports to North America would increase by $17 to $19 billion, giving annual rates of 15 percent to 17 percent.

A major implication is a widening of the non-oil trade deficit. Only market mechanisms can be relied upon to finance such a gap, and in the framework of North American integration, both foreign direct investment (of $5 billion annually) and capital repatriation (which may take the form of short-term funds in the range of $3 to $5 billion) are feasible, ignoring factors such as capital scarcity provoked by Eastern European events or a deep U.S. recession. Provided such inflows of capital can be induced, the high level of imports can be sustained by additional borrowing, although further relief of debt service costs may also become necessary. The current account deficit would be $8.9 to $15.0 billion during the first three years of the FTA. Higher deficits projected in the fourth and fifth years may not be sustainable or may require a reduction in interest on the foreign debt or additional borrowing. But even for the first three years, the FTA will require a maximum opening of Mexican industry to foreign investment and capital inflows. In terms of GDP, it will represent between 3.8 percent and 5.8 percent including debt service during the first three years, but only between 1.0 percent and 3.3 percent excluding debt service. The projected levels of imports, the current account deficit, and further borrowing requirements leave no doubt that the effects of North American economic integration would reinforce themselves: an FTA leading to increased investment and trade flows would call in due time for greater liberalization of investment.

Adjustment costs for Mexican industry will be important in the short run and have been estimated at 0.5 percent of GDP per annum over the next five years. In a policy framework, these costs are relatively unimportant. One reason is that a large part of the adjustment costs have already been absorbed by the Mexican economy in anticipation of the FTA, while most of the benefits are still to be realized. These costs result from the reduction in tariffs that Mexico undertook unilaterally in 1985-90. The benefits will accrue when North America reduces its tariffs and non-tariff barriers to Mexican exports. Although Mexico will have to reciprocate with additional reductions, these will be small compared to the reductions effected in past years.

Economic integration with North America would be inevitable if the decision depended entirely on market forces. Nevertheless, governments will be able to influence its completeness and its pace and could give different forms to such integration. It is desirable that they ensure maximum market access and promote institutional changes to facilitate a quick adjustment with minimum uncertainty.

Appendix

The model used to simulate effects includes only a few variables. The rate of gross fixed investment (dI) is determined exogenously according to the need to raise output per worker in Mexico. Export growth (dX) results from $1 billion of annual exports gained from trade diversion added to increases in the present level of Mexican exports. Growth in non-oil exports depends on the rate of growth in North America (dUY), for which we use the U.S. GDP growth as a proxy and changes in the real exchange rate of the peso (dR). Oil exports are assumed to be exogenous. A variable denoting changes in the productivity of capital (dPK) is used to complete the explanation of GDP growth, which is made to depend on changes in manufacturing employment (dE) and in non-oil exports. In other words, higher employment reflects more optimum levels of industrial capacity, while exports force firms to seek greater efficiency and smoother production runs. Employment growth depends on the level of capacity utilization, approximated as the ratio of current manufacturing output to the trough level of 1983-1 (MP). Thus,

$$dY = f(dYt\text{-}1, dI, dPK, dX) \tag{1}$$

$$dX = f(dUY, dR) \tag{2}$$

$$dPK = f(dE, dX) \tag{3}$$

$$dE = f(MP) \tag{4}$$

Growth of imports (dM) depend on GDP growth (dY) and the real exchange rate changes. The growth in productivity of labour (dPL) is estimated as a function of investment growth (dI), import growth (dM), and the change in the rate of growth of capacity utilization (DMP). This is measured as a multiple of the current level of manufacturing output over the trough in 1983-1. Nevertheless, dPL does not enter as an independent variable into any of the estimated equations.

$$dM = f(dY, dR) \tag{5}$$

$$dPL = f(dI, dM, dDMP) \tag{6}$$

Regression equations with monthly data for the period 1983-1 to the period 1989-12 were estimated in order to determine the significance of the relationships postulated above. Monthly data are not fully adequate for these purposes since, among other things, they embody seasonality in the output series. Moreover, a lack of monthly GDP data obliged an interpolation from quarterly series. Although annual data would have corrected part of these problems, there would not have been enough observations, given that trade liberalization essentially commenced in 1985. Therefore, the results reported below are only crude estimates, and in some cases the relationships obtained are very poor. Nevertheless, on the whole they consistently show correct signs and statistical significance. All equations were estimated in natural log form with variables expressed as either physical volumes or current values deflated by the relevant price indices.

(1) Imports (M)

$$M = -16.86^* + 4.37\,Y^* - 0.26\,R^*$$

(t values) (-7.7) (8.68) (-1.85)

$R2=0.81$ $DW=0.64$ $F=113.32$

(2) Non-oil exports (X)

$$X = -39.43^* + 5.04\,UY^* + 0.68R^*$$

(-15.36) (16.0) (5.34)

$R2=0.91$ $DW=0.73$ $F=285.38$

(3) $Y = 1.12^* + 0.46\,Yt\text{-}1^* + 0.31\,I^* + 0.21\,PK^*$

(3.88) (7.70) (9.56) (4.26)

$R2=0.81$ $DW=0.96$ $F=77.19$

(4) $PL = -1.04^* + 0.2096I^* + 0.0707M^* + 0.0021DMP$

(-5.38) (4.11) (2.42) (0.39)

$R2\ 0.63$ $DW=0.84...F=45.20$

(5) $E = 3.3325^* + 0.2657MP^*$

(20.95) (7.41)

$R2 =0.75$ $DW=0.54$ $F=123.0$

(6) $PK = -1.2252 + 0.3153E + 0.0646\,X^*$

(-0.88) (1.02) (2.41)

$R2 =0.63$ $DW=0.84$ $F = 12.74$

* statistically significant at the 99 percent level.

References

Clavijo Fernando and Faini Riccardo, *Las elasticidades ingreso ciclicas y seculares de la demanda de importaciones en los paises en desarrollo*, El Trimestre Economico, Vol. 57 (1), Mexico, enero-marzo 1990, No. 225.

van Wijnbergen, Sweder, *Trade reform, policy uncertainty and the current account: a non-expected utility approach*, London: Centre for Economic Policy Research, Discussion Paper Series, No. 441, August 1990.

Chapter 2

A Canadian Vision of North American Economic Integration

Leonard Waverman

Introduction

Canada and Mexico have never had significant trade, investment, or political ties, and at this point both countries appear unsure of what role they can play in North America together. The absence of political ties between the two nations is most surprising since, as I'll show below, their relationships with the.U.S. have much in common. Now they have the opportunity to reach out and form close ties.

In 1989 there was a minimal relationship between Canada and Mexico. Mexican trade with Canada involved $1.68 billion of Mexican exports and $1.0 billion of Canadian exports. Canada is Mexico's 11th largest trading partner and Mexico is Canada's 17th largest trading partner. For Mexico, Canada's trade is less important than Japan, Germany, or France. For Canada, trade with Mexico is small compared to trade with South Korea, Taiwan, France, or Italy. Canadian direct foreign investment in Mexico is $400 million, while there is no Mexican investment in Canada to speak of. The absence of trade and investment flows between Canada and Mexico is surely a motivation for a free trade agreement, not an excuse to avoid it. The economic gains in trade between Canada and Mexico will involve the traditional ones of exercising comparative advantage and using Canadian expertise to rebuild Mexico. Other economic gains include the rationalization of North American industry on a continental basis and making the region stronger in the face of regional blocks being developed in Europe and Asia.

A free trade agreement also provides significant political advantages to Mexico and Canada because together they can offset protectionist measures in the U.S.: the U.S. will not be able to play one country against the other. Canada has had an uneasy relationship with the world's most powerful nation, since power is naturally viewed apprehensively in any bilateral context. The inclusion of Mexico in a trilateral relationship and extension of the Canada-U.S. Free Trade Agreement (CAFTA) to other countries in the Western Hemisphere and to other relationships beyond trade in goods and some services is of great value to Canada.

Though political developments in Canada are not propitious at this time for an outward vision to Mexico, I provide justification for such a vision, arguing that movement to a "common market" in North America is a beneficial long-term strategy.

Canada's Trade and Foreign Investment Regimes: An Uneasy Relationship with the U.S.

In 1988 trade between Canada and the U.S. amounted to $30 billion U.S., the world's largest bilateral trade flow and one where 80 percent of the goods crossed the Canada-U.S. border duty free. Yet Canada and the U.S. negotiated a free trade agreement in the late 1980s—why was such a treaty necessary?

The Free Trade Agreement between Canada and the U.S. that came into effect on January 1, 1989, was the third such agreement negotiated or discussed in detail by the two countries, but the first ratified[1] (the other two were in 1911 and 1948, the decision to end discussions was taken by Canada). In the past, Canada was reluctant to rely on market forces to determine trade with the U.S., and this led to a set of policies—barriers to trade in goods and services, impediments to foreign-direct investment, preferences for Canadian-owned companies, and reliance on multilateral (GATT) initiatives. Thus, while most trade in goods between Canada and the U.S. was duty free in 1988, even in the 1980s Canadian constraints on the movement of certain goods (e.g., energy) had been tight, significant barriers existed in trade in services, and cross-border capital flows into Canada required prior approval. An intergovernmental agreement to allow duty-free movement across the border existed only for the automobile industry. Although the existence of this pact was longstanding

---

1   In 1854, 13 years before Canadian Confederation, the U.S. and Canadian colonies entered into the Reciprocity Treaty, which allowed free trade for a variety of primary products. The treaty was terminated by the U.S. in 1866.

(since 1965) and successful,[2] no bilateral agreement existed for trade in other goods or services.

Other Canadian policies were put in place to limit dependence on the U.S. In 1973 foreign ownership of the Canadian manufacturing sector was 51 percent, and in the Canadian petroleum industry it was 79 percent. In 1974 the Foreign Investment Review Agency was established to determine whether acquisitions of Canadian business were in the national interest. A federal Crown corporation (Petro-Canada) was established in the hydrocarbon sector in 1975 and various fiscal incentives were given to Canadian controlled petroleum companies. In addition, limits on oil exports to the U.S. were introduced.

These Canadian policies had their parallels in Mexico, although Mexican policies and controls were far more extreme than those in Canada. In 1973 the Mexican government introduced new legislation on foreign ownership with the Law to Promote Mexican Investment and Regulate Foreign Investment; limits on oil exports to the U.S. were announced in the mid-1970s and the oil industry had been nationalized since 1938. With these fears of U.S. dominance, it is unclear why so little contact developed between Canada and Mexico.

Canadian policy tried to diversify trade away from the U.S. market. Canada played a leading role in the Kennedy and Tokyo GATT rounds. This emphasis on multilateralism was due to the belief (common to smaller countries) that a multinational approach limits the potential for one large country to exploit its relationship with a smaller country. In the GATT, the U.S. is but one of many voices (though significant).

The result of the large multilateral trade liberalization in successive GATT rounds was, however, a growing concentration of Canadian trade with the U.S. This did not and does not mean that multilateralism has failed Canada. On the contrary, multilateral negotiations give smaller countries such as Canada (and Mexico) plural partners to combat the clear market power of large countries. A multilateral rules-based mechanism for codifying trade and trade disputes, and for providing global reductions in tariff barriers, is clearly in Canadian interests.

Besides these multilateral approaches, Canada has had significant trade and investment relationships with other countries and regions. Canada is a part of the British Commonwealth and, until British entry into the European Commu-

---

2   In 1961 Canadian domestic automobile production consisted of 327,000 vehicles spread over 49 nameplates. Costs were high (an efficient scale plant in this period is estimated to have produced 400,000 to 800,000 cars per annum). Little trade occurred. Canadian/U.S. exports/imports in 1961 were 107,000 and 9,500 cars respectively. In 1989 Canada imported 632,000 cars and exported 1,196,000 cars to the U.S. Cross-border auto parts trade totalled $32 billion CDN.

nity in 1973, Canada enjoyed significant preferential access to the U.K. market. In 1950 the U.K. was the source of 12.7 percent of Canadian imports and the market for 15.1 percent of Canadian exports (as compared to 67.1 percent and 64.8 percent, respectively, for the U.S.). In 1950 U.K. residents were the owners of 20 percent of Canadian foreign direct investment (as compared to 75.6 percent for the U.S.). In 1969 Prime Minister Trudeau made a conscious attempt to diversify Canadian trade away from the U.S. by launching a European initiative. Ten years after this initiative began, trade between Canada and the EC had diminished from 14.6 percent to 9.3 percent of total Canadian trade while trade between Canada and the U.S. had stayed fairly constant.

Thus, in the mid-1980s Canadian trade was concentrated in the U.S. market. These two countries enjoyed the largest bilateral trade flow in the world. However, the Canadian government became increasingly concerned that Canadian exports to the U.S. were at risk due to two fundamental problems—first, a perception that the Canadian manufacturing industry was not at efficient world scale levels, and second, that Canadian exports to the U.S., primarily but not exclusively the products of secondary manufacturing, would be subject to growing U.S. protectionism.

In the 1980s there was a growing use (abuse to some authors) of contingent trade protection in the U.S. against Canadian firms (see Rugman and Verbeke, 1989). Canadian producers began to feel that a protectionist Congress and the ability of U.S. manufacturing firms to effectively use countervail proceedings against Canadian producers meant that the world's largest undefended border could see trade fences erected. Therefore, there was overwhelming business support (including smaller and medium-sized companies) for a free trade agreement with the U.S.

The Canada-U.S. Free Trade Agreement of 1989

On January 1, 1989, the Canada-United States Free Trade Agreement (CAFTA) came into effect.

> The FTA is the most comprehensive and far-reaching trade agreement ever signed between two sovereign nations. It establishes a coherent and binding framework of rules tailored to the trade and investment realities of the 1990s by:
> - *completing* the process of trade liberalization begun between Canada and the United States with the bilateral agreements of

1935 and 1938 and continued through the GATT, the Autopact and the defence production sharing arrangements[3]
- *continuing* the process of bilateral rule-making begun in 1935
- *establishing* for the first time a bilateral, contractual institutional basis for the management of the bilateral trade and economic relationship
- *introducing* the rule of nondiscrimination to the new frontiers of trade policy such as trade in services and investment...(Hart, 1989).

Notwithstanding Hart's assessment of the enormous strides made in CAFTA, the agreement is not anywhere near the multilateral free trade enjoyed by the European Community (EC); Canada and the U.S. are far from comprehensive economic integration. In particular, there are a number of important issues not covered in the 1989 agreement:

1. CAFTA is not an agreement liberalizing trade in all goods
   a) certain goods are only covered peripherally—agriculture
   b) trade in certain goods is constrained—textiles
   c) certain goods are excluded—beer
2. CAFTA is only the beginning of an agreement covering trade in services:
   a) certain services are explicitly excluded: basic telecommunications; transportation; culture; media; doctors, dentists, lawyers; and child care.
   b) trade in certain services is constrained since existing discrimination is grandfathered—financial services.
3. Investment
   a) most service sectors are included except financial services, transportation, Crown corporations, and investment related to government procurement
   b) the review of foreign investment by Investment Canada is liberalized for U.S. firms but not for other countries

---

3 The 1935 and 1938 agreements are available as No. 9 (1936) and No. 8 (1939), respectively, in the Canada Treaty Series. The original General Agreement on Tariffs and Trade (GATT) and related documents suspending the 1938 Canada-U.S. agreement can be found as No. 27 and 27A (1947) in that same series and has been periodically reissued as a result of revisions. The 1965 Autopact is No. 14 (1966). The Defence Production Sharing Arrangements are contained in a series of agreements, letters, and understandings dating back to the 1941 Hyde Park Declaration issued by President Roosevelt and Prime Minister King.

4. CAFTA is not an agreement liberalizing trade in factors, in particular, labour movements are not allowed except for certain limited circumstances.
5. CAFTA does not allow the free movement of goods since each country can still impose contingent protection measures (countervail and anti-dump) against imports from the other. In fact, the number of contingent protection cases between the U.S. and Canada rose in 1989.

There are other features of potential economic integration not included in the CAFTA:

6. The U.S. and Canada retain individual barriers (tariff and non-tariff) against third countries. When a free trade association also includes common external barriers, it can be classified as a *customs union*.

Lipsey and Smith wrote that "a common trade policy against nonmembers would be unacceptable to Canadians" (1985, p. 77). However, in the longer term, pressures to harmonize many external barriers between Canada and the U.S. are clearly evident. A good example is in the automotive sector where Canada retains a significantly higher barrier to imports of vehicles and parts than the U.S. (6 percent vs. 2 percent tariffs). Thus, a foreign firm not able to achieve duty-free access to the North American market but wishing to import components to assemble cars, faces higher costs in Canada than in the U.S. In the past Canada had been able to offer duty remission schemes to offset this disadvantage, but these schemes are to be eliminated in CAFTA. Thus, pressure exists to reduce the Canadian tariff to U.S. levels.

7. As noted, CAFTA does not allow labour mobility, nor is there complete freedom for capital flows. Thus, Canada and the U.S. do not enjoy a common market, as do the 12 members of the European Community.

Comparisons with Europe

Starting from a background of startling differences and enormous animosities, Europe is proceeding to economic union and some form of political union. This sweeping change began in 1952 when six nations—Belgium, France, Italy, Luxembourg, West Germany, and The Netherlands—formed the European Steel and Coal Community. These six also formed the European Economic Community in 1958, which expanded to nine nations in 1973 with the entry of Britain, Denmark, and the Irish Republic, to ten in 1981 (Greece), and 12 in 1986 (Spain and Portugal). The U.S. and Canada, with little animosity and many similarities, have been discussing free trade for over 135 years!

There is no simple reason why a group of 12 different and bellicose nations can achieve in 30 years what the U.S. and Canada have not achieved in 135 years. However, the diversity of language and culture in Europe, as well as the large number of member countries, makes economic and political union easier in Europe since cultural identity is not directly threatened. Much of Canada shares an identical language and a similar culture with the U.S., which is an industrial and political giant. Therefore, a common market has been unthinkable to Canadians. Many Canadians feel they would be submerged by the U.S., as the similarities and the overwhelming size of its southern neighbour would force Canada into the position of a state, and not the most important one either. These fears prevent the formation of a common market between Canada and the U.S., a market whose benefits the Europeans have enjoyed for a number of years.

However, the willingness of Mexico's 82 million people (by 2000, 100 million, or 40 percent of the size of the U.S.) and the beginnings of a U.S. examination of hemispheric free trade, make a North, Central, and South American common market a long-term reality for Canada.

The addition of Mexico to some form of CAFTA would alleviate all ancillary problems that an unequal-size, two-party game leads to by making it a three-party game. I have shown that Canada and Mexico have many similarities, as they must given their sharing North America with the world's greatest economic and political power. In the past, Canada and Mexico have totally ignored their relationship and joint interests. A North American free trade agreement allows them to build that relationship. The existence of two parallel trade accords—U.S.-Mexico (MUFTA) and CAFTA will have the opposite effect—Canada and Mexico will become economic and political adversaries rather than the political friends that they should be. Thus, a North America free trade agreement gives Canada political as well as economic advantages.

Historically, Canada has had an ambivalent attitude towards the U.S. While Canada has become increasingly economically integrated with the U.S., it has continued to be wary of such integration and has sought to contain it through tariffs, foreign investment review, specific sectoral policies (such as energy), and multilateralism. The CAFTA is an important step for Canada towards economic integration with the U.S. This step, while enormously significant, still leaves Canada and the U.S. far from a common market. A North American or Northern Hemisphere trade agreement could be in keeping with Canada's multilateral desires. In particular, an agreement involving Mexico and Canada should increase Canada's negotiating strength with the U.S.

Trade Flows

Table 1 provides a schematic overview of the trade flows among the three countries, as well as their trade with the rest of the world (ROW).[4] In 1987 the U.S. imported nearly $71 billion worth of goods and services from Canada, $18.7 billion from Mexico, and $316 billion from ROW—for a total of $405 billion. Canadian imports represented 12.5 percent of U.S. imports (by far the largest single country); Mexico was the third largest exporter to the U.S. (4.6 percent of U.S. imports).[5] U.S. exports to Canada were $57 billion; to Mexico, $14.6 billion; and to ROW, $178.5 billion. Both Canada and Mexico had current account surpluses with the U.S.: $13.5 billion and $4.3 billion, respectively.

Mexico and Canada have remarkably similar trade patterns with the U.S. In 1987 the U.S. was the destination of 69.7 percent of Mexican exports and 77.9 percent of Canadian exports, and the source of 74.3 percent of Mexican imports and 67.2 percent of Canadian imports. In 1987 Canada and Mexico were dependent on the U.S., as a market and as a source of imports, for roughly two-thirds to three-quarters of their trade.

As noted at the outset, Mexico and Canada are not important trading partners. Mexico is the destination for less than half of 1 percent of Canadian exports; Mexican exports represent 1.0 percent of all Canadian imports. Since Mexican trade is so much smaller than Canadian trade, the Canadian market accounts for 3.3 percent of Mexican exports.

Table 2 provides a slightly more detailed breakdown of trade flows between the three countries, with trade classified into four categories: resource-intensive products (animals, beverages, crude materials, etc.); primary manufacturing (manufactured goods by chief material—iron and steel, aluminium smelting, etc.); the machinery and transport equipment sectors; and all other secondary manufacturing.

In 1988-89 47 percent of Canadian exports and 33 percent of Mexican exports to the U.S. consisted of resource or primary manufactured products. Nearly 60 percent of Canadian exports to Mexico were resource or primary manufactured products, while nearly 70 percent of Mexican exports to Canada consisted of secondary manufactured products; 72 percent of U.S. exports to Canada and Mexico were from secondary manufacturing.

---

4 Mexican exports from the in-bond border assembly factories (maquiladoras) are not shown; the value added from their activities was some $2.3 billion in 1988.

5 Japan was the second largest importer to the U.S. in 1987, at $28.25 billion (7 percent of U.S. total imports).

Table 1
North American Trade Flows 1987 U.S. Dollars (Billions)

EXPORTS	IMPORTS					
	U.S.	Canada	Mexico	ROW	Trade Total	Balance
U.S.	—	57.36	14.58	178.45	250.39	-154.82
Canada	70.78	—	0.40	25.85	97.03	111.72
Mexico—non-oil	13.96	0.75	—	4.60	19.31	7.17
—oil	4.70	0.14	—	2.43	7.27	—
ROW	315.77	27.06	4.63			
Total	405.21	85.31	19.61			

North American Trade Flows—Percentages—1987
Exports, (Imports)

	U.S.	Canada	Mexico	ROW
U.S.—exports to	—	23	5.8	71.2
—imports from	—	(17.5)	(4.6)	(77.9)
Canada—exports to	72.9	—	0.4	26.7
—imports from	(67.2)	—	(1.0)	(31.8)
Mexico—exports to	69.7	3.3	—	26.9
—imports from	(74.3)	(2.0)	—	(23.6)

Source: Cline, 1989, pp. 142, 143.

Table 2
1988/89 Trade Patterns (Percentage of Total Trade)
Between Canada, United States, and Mexico
(Goods)

	C/U	M/U	U/C	U/M	C/M	M/C
Resources	16.4%	23.5%	8.2%	17.4%	32.7%	11.6%
Primary	30.8	9.7	19.9	11.0	26.9	19.5
Machinery and transport equip.	46.0	49.1	60.4	49.0	35.6	65.2
Other Secon. Manufac.	6.8	17.7	11.5	22.6	4.8	3.7

C: Canada
U: U.S.
M: Mexico

Source: Waverman, 1990.

The pattern that emerges is one of Canadian exports of resource, primary, and secondary manufactured materials being exchanged for other primary materials, but mainly for secondary manufactured goods. Mexican exports of secondary manufactured goods represent goods with a high component of low-skilled assembly labour.[6]

In another work (Waverman, 1990) I attempted to characterize the 1987 trade between each pair of countries as predominantly "inter-industry" (arising from specialization and comparative advantage[7]) or "intra-industry" (arising from firms' advantages, economies of scale, and product differentiation). That analysis indicated that trade between Canada and the U.S. was primarily intra-industry; Mexican-U.S. trade was a mixture of intra-industry (the two-way trade in manufactured goods) and inter-industry trade (shipments of resources and food), while Canada-Mexico trade was far more inter-industry than U.S.-Mexico (or Canada-U.S.) trade.

The intra-industry trade between Canada and the U.S. reflects similar technology and uses of factors of production (land, labour, capital, resources) in two highly developed economies. The inter-industry trade between Mexico and Canada reflects the sharp differences in technology and factors of production in the two economies.

A free trade agreement between Mexico, the U.S., and Canada would expand this trade to predominately one of Mexican high-labour content, secondary manufactured goods, and resource products for U.S. and Canadian products. What are the economic benefits (and costs) to Canada of such trade?

---

6 Mexico has made enormous strides in recent years in raising the skill level of employees and producing more complex quality products.

7 Comparative advantage is defined as the international advantage a country has in one industry relative to a second industry. Comparative advantage should not be confused (as it often is) with absolute advantage—the fact that one country may have lower costs of production than another country in a specific industry. The pattern of trade is not determined by absolute advantage but by comparative advantage. "An absolute advantage over other countries in producing a good is neither necessary nor sufficient to yield comparative advantage in that good." (Krugman and Obstfeld, 1988, p. 25). A country can have an absolute advantage over another country in all goods, yet two-way trade will exist and make both countries better off. This is not a paradox when one realizes that what determines the trade is the relative or comparative advantage between two industries in the two countries. It pays the country with absolute advantage to specialize in the product it is *comparatively* best at, and trade that for other products. This specialization will lead to higher welfare than autarky when a country produces all goods domestically.

The Impacts of Free Trade Agreements

There are many interrelated effects of trade liberalization on Canadian welfare. These consist of three types of impacts: first, the classical impacts of trade creation, trade diversion, and changes in the terms of trade; second, the impacts resulting from assumptions that manufacturing industries are not perfectly competitive and operate under conditions of increasing returns to scale; and third, the so called "dynamic effects" (Lipsey and Smith, 1985, p. 42) not captured in the quantitative estimates. It is useful to briefly summarize these effects.

Trade Creation

Removing barriers to trade improves the allocation of resources in an economy. Resources are reallocated through trade creation and trade diversion. Both of these impact on the degree and type of industry specialization and on the terms of trade received by an industry. The "terms of trade" refers to the amount of imports received for a given amount of exports. It can be thought of as the relative price of exports for imports.

Imagine two industries, A and B, perfectly competitive and operating in each of the two countries, but with tariffs levelled at each border. Without the tariffs, the Canadian firms in industry A could have sold in the U.S. at lower prices than U.S. domestic producers (say the industry is one in which Canada is naturally favoured, i.e., Canada has a comparative advantage in A). Similarly, after the bilateral removal of tariffs, U.S. producers in industry B could underprice Canadian producers in the Canadian market. Before tariff removal, prices were raised in both countries because of the presence of tariffs. As a result of bilateral tariff removal, Canada specializes in its comparative advantage—industry A, the U.S. specializes in industry B in which it has a comparative advantage, and trade increases (there was none before the tariffs were removed). Prices in both countries fall. Through such international specialization, world welfare increases since each country's resources are devoted to the activity in which it has a comparative advantage—the stock of resources (land, labour, and capital) in the two countries produces more output after the tariffs are removed so that comparative advantage can be utilized. With increased specialization will come increased incomes and therefore a potential for increased imports as well.

Trade Diversion

Let us complicate the example by including other countries in the U.S. market. Assume that Canada is but one of two exporters to the U.S. in industry A. Both exporters to the U.S. face the same level of tariffs, but country M exports more to the U.S. than Canada as it has somewhat lower costs. After a bilateral free trade agreement including Canada and the U.S. but excluding country M, Canadian exports to the U.S. increase at the expense of country M since M's exports continue to incur the tariff while Canada's exports do not. This is trade diversion to Canada's benefit but at the expense of other exporters to the U.S. market (see Lipsey and Smith, 1985, p. 41). This example makes it clear that the CAFTA led to trade diversion for Canada at the expense of Mexico.

Trade diversion is an important source of gains to Canada in the empirical economics literature examining the costs and benefits of CAFTA. For example, Cox and Harris (1986) reported that Canada-U.S. bilateral free trade would lead to a large 9.0 percent gain in Canadian welfare:

> As the small country in the arrangement, Canada benefits by the diversion of U.S. trade from other countries towards Canada. Given the existence of scale economies in Canadian industries, the larger market afforded by the diversion of U.S. imports towards Canada clearly benefits Canada. The extent of the diversion of trade within Canada is reported by the U.S. trade index. This reports the proportion of total Canadian trade accounted for by the United States. In the base equilibrium 71 per cent of Canadian trade is with the United States. Under BFT [bilateral free trade] this figure increased to 76 per cent. The trade expansion effect of the free-trade area is quite substantial. Under BFT the volume of total trade increases by over 87 per cent. The volume of trade with the United States increases by over 97 per cent (pp. 386-87).

An analysis of trade agreements with Mexico must include an examination of the loss of trade diversion benefits enjoyed by Canada in its preferential trade agreement with the U.S. where Mexican industry shares preferential access in U.S. markets with Canadian industry.

Terms of Trade

If we complicate the model even further by allowing some trade with the existence of tariffs, then lowering tariffs changes the "terms of trade," the relative price, or the real exchange rate between imports and exports. The magnitude of the terms of trade effect (or even its direction) depends on the assumptions one makes about how a country's exports or imports effect the price in the other country. In most analyses of CAFTA, the "Canada as a small country" assumption was made. This assumes that Canada as a small country cannot affect world prices for products.[8] Thus, terms of trade effects were considered minimal by some researchers examining CAFTA. A similar assumption can be made for Mexico—it is unlikely that Mexican production will affect prices in the U.S. or Canada.

Economies of Scale, Productivity, and Competition

The very large gains to Canada accruing from a CAFTA in the Cox-Harris results mentioned above do not result from "simple" trade creation or trade diversion. Instead, the welfare gains to Canada are due to two interrelated effects. First are the lower production costs in Canadian industry arising from the economies of scale resulting from larger markets; second, increased competitiveness in the Canadian market lowers the profit mark-up by domestic Canadian industries and this lower price also increases the volume produced. The estimates of trade diversion in the U.S. (the gains in Canadian exports at the expense of third countries) is largely due to the beneficial impacts of scale and competition for Canadian industry.

Obviously, in analyzing the economic impacts of trade agreements on Mexico, the issues of the capture of scale economies are crucial. What percentages of the reductions in costs are translated into price decreases and the impact of increased import competition on prices depends on the assumptions made about the nature of competition.[9]

Three types of competition are important. First, the impact of new competition in the Mexican market from U.S. (and Canadian) producers and exporters; second, the competition between Mexican and Canadian producers in U.S. markets, and third, the increased competition in Canadian markets from Mexican producers. From the Canadian perspective, these three issues are important

---

8   The small country assumption is that Canada imports from the U.S. at the U.S. price (plus tariff) and exports to the U.S. at the world price (U.S. customers pay the world price plus the U.S. tariff). One could also argue that when a CAFTA is introduced, the price in Canada falls by the amount of the Canadian tariff. The price received by Canadian exporters rises to the level of the U.S. domestic price (which includes a tariff against third countries now not levelled against Canadians). Canadian welfare through the terms of trade effect is positive; however, U.S. welfare falls. Alternatively, the term of trade effect can be negative for Canada (as it is in Wigle, 1988) if the world price is depressed by the high Canadian tariff; lowering that tariff raises U.S. prices.

9   In the case of analyzing CAFTA, researchers disagreed as to the exact pricing rule to model, but they did agree as to the importance of the assumptions used (see Wigle, 1988; Brown and Stern, 1987; Harris, 1987).

since increased competition in Mexico can lead to lower prices in Mexico, rationalization, greater exports, and increased competition in both the U.S. and Canadian markets. Therefore, a complete analysis of the economic impacts of new trade pacts on Canada must include an analysis of the degree to which Canadian and Mexican goods do and will compete.

Dynamic Gains

Richard Lipsey and Murray Smith (1985) list four beneficial dynamic effects of a CAFTA on the Canadian economy.

- It would force private-sector firms to drop inefficient practices, built up behind tariff walls;
- It would promote through trade creation the transfer of resources from potentially declining industries to potentially expanding industries;
- It would reduce the government's temptation to continue to subsidize declining industries; and
- "It would allow Canadian firms to introduce new products and to participate early in emerging industries because of free access to large, high income markets" (pp. 42, 43).

To these gains a fifth can be added, one discussed as very important in the case of Mexico (see Weintraub, 1989):

- Free trade areas remove much of the rent-seeking activities of business where resources are spent in gaining protection rather than in learning to compete.

A sixth element can be very important when trade liberalization leads to sharp gains in growth for one of the countries, as will likely be the case for Mexico in a North American trade pact—I call this the "growth dividend."

Growth Dividend

The U.S. and Canada are large, highly developed economies. While a free trade agreement between them yielded net benefits (dispersed more to Canada, the smaller economy), a change in the basic nature of either country was not expected. Thus, at the margin the gains to each country do not lead to substantial gains for the other. Mexico, however, is an underdeveloped economy, by definition one which has the capacity for enormous change and enormous growth. If Mexico does achieve its potential because of its association with the rest of North America, Mexican growth will be far above that experienced in the U.S. and will spill over to the other two economies leading to a growth dividend.

Estimate of Costs and Benefits to Canada of Liberalized Trade with Mexico

I assume the possibility of two very different agreements. The first is a broad Mexico-U.S. free trade agreement (MUFTA) in which Canada is not included. This agreement would include across the board reciprocal tariff removal over time plus some bilateral agreement on investment whereby existing Mexican stringent rules on foreign ownership would be loosened for U.S. firms. Thus, Mexican firms would be given equal preferential access in U.S. markets with Canadian firms.

Alternatively, one can consider such a broad agreement among Canada, the U.S., and Mexico—a North America free trade agreement (NAFTA).

In other work (Waverman, 1990) I have estimated the trade losses for Canada under a MUFTA and a NAFTA. Here I summarize those results under nine sources of welfare (Canadian domestic production) change.

Static Trade Diversion: U.S. Market

MUFTA

Canada must lose exports to the U.S. under a MUFTA. The reasoning is simple. A MUFTA lowers the prices of Mexican goods in U.S. markets (the cost of the U.S. tariff). Therefore Mexican goods become cheaper relative to Canadian goods in those segments where Mexico and Canada compete. The Mexican Ministry of Finance (SECOFI) estimated the trade diversion losses for Mexico which resulted from the CAFTA, since that agreement lowered the price of Canadian goods relative to Mexican goods. These losses were near $500 million U.S. or 7 percent of 1989 Mexican exports to the U.S.

Using two existing sets of estimates of cross-price elasticities (the responsiveness of Canadian exports to changes in the price of Mexican goods in U.S. markets), I estimate that only minor trade diversion occurs for Canada from a MUFTA, some $100 million (or less than 1/7 of 1 percent of 1989 Canadian exports to the U.S.). This value is given in the first line of table 3.

This is likely a substantial underestimate of Canada's trade diversion loss for a number of reasons. First, Mexican exports are clearly changing and growing rapidly (without any trade pact), thus using the past as a guide (and the above estimates use the pre-1987 past as a guide) is clearly inadequate.[10] Second, and similar to the first point, secure access to the U.S. market could lead to shifts in resources in Mexico to export oriented sectors, and this could

---

10 Mexican exports are not near any equilibrium state.

Table 3
Incremental Costs and Benefits to Canada
From Trade Pacts with Mexico
Measured as changes in Domestic Canadian Production
(U.S. $, millions)

		MUFTA	NAFTA
1.	Trade Diversion—U.S. Market	- 100	- 100
2.	Trade Diversion—Mexican Market	- 21	0
3.	Trade Creation—Mexican Market		
	Direct	0	+ 93
	Indirect	0	+ 76
4.	Production Losses—Canadian Market	—	- 125
5.	Specialization Gains—Canadian Market	—	+
6.	Terms of Trade Effects	0	0
7.	Economies of Scale and Productivity		
	Changes—Canada	—	+
8.	Dynamic Gains	0	+
9.	Growth Dividend (1993-1995 Average)	+ 220	+ 600

See text for sources of estimates.

be to Canada's disadvantage. Third, much of the Canadian "gains from trade" estimated to occur with a CAFTA were due to the capture of economies of scale and resulting productivity improvements; therefore, increased Mexican access to U.S. markets will expand the scale of Mexican production, lowering costs and prices. Thus, competition between Mexico and Canada in the U.S. market will likely increase.

Several points, however, suggest that this process will not lead to very large trade diversion losses for Canada. This process of gaining scale and productivity and consequent cost reductions for Mexican industry is an experience already gained in many countries—Korea, Taiwan, Thailand, Singapore, Hong Kong, and especially Japan. While these countries have experienced enormous gains in their exports of secondary manufacturing, Canadian exports, including exports of secondary manufacturing sector, have continued to increase[11] as the table below shows. In the thirteen-year period from 1975 to 1988, Japanese

11 Surely, had these countries not developed, then Canadian exports would have increased even more.

exports to the U.S. increased by $78 billion. However Canadian exports to the U.S. increased by $59 billion.

Table 4
Increases in Exports to the U.S.
1975-88

FROM:	Canada	Japan	Korea
Total percentage increase	265%	686%	1300%
Change in $value (U.S.$)	58751	78377	18747

Source: The Statistical Abstract of the United States, U.S. Department of Commerce (1978, 1990).

The point is that Canada continues to face new competition all the time. Mexican economic expansion will provide more competition. A free trade agreement between Mexico and the U.S. will provide Mexican industry with secure access to the U.S. market, a degree of access not granted to Korea or Japan.

A sector-by-sector analysis of Mexican and Canadian industry is required but unavailable. Several key sectors can be cursorily surveyed. In textiles and steel Mexican and Canadian (as well as all other) exports to the U.S. are set by quotas (for textiles under the Multifibre Agreement and CAFTA; for steel under the U.S. Voluntary Restraint Agreement). Since these quotas, not competition, limit Canadian exports, an increase in Mexican exports will not come at the expense of Canadian sales to the U.S. A most important sector is automobile assembly and parts production. Canada and the U.S. have had a form of free trade in automotive products since 1965; the U.S. and Mexico have had a form of free trade in auto parts for many years (the maquiladora program).[12] As a result, auto parts now move quite freely across North America. However, a MUFTA or NAFTA will allow for the nationalization of Mexican domestic automobile assembly and associated auto parts production. It is these longer term investments that could alter the North American automobile industry. How much assembly and parts production will shift to Mexico is unknown. The most informed estimate (Womack et al., 1990) sees major investments in the Mexican automobile sector but at the expense of Asian production, not Canada or

---

12 The maquiladora program utilizes the sections of the U.S. tariff code that allow the export and re-import of U.S.-made components further assembled in countries such as Mexico where U.S. tariffs are levied only on the value-added in these countries.

U.S. production. In any event, what is crucial for Canada is incremental protection resulting from Canada's staying out of trade pacts with Mexico—in my view there is little such protection. A trade pact between Mexico and the U.S. with Canada explicitly excluded provides most of the increased competition that Canadians seem to fear.

NAFTA

What trade diversion losses for Canada occur in U.S. markets when a tripartite North American free trade agreement is formed? The answer is obvious—the exact same trade diversion losses in U.S. markets estimated above for a MUFTA. The reason is clear. Does adding Canada to a Mexico-U.S. trade agreement alter the competition between Canada and Mexico in U.S. markets? Given the existence of CAFTA, clearly not. Note one additional important point. Were Canada not already in a trade agreement with the U.S., a MUFTA could lead to substantial trade diversion losses for Canada—additional motivations for CAFTA. Fortunately, CAFTA already exists!

Therefore, in table 3, identical static trade diversion losses are estimated for Canada for both sets of agreements.

Static Trade Diversion: Mexican Market

MUFTA

Following a MUFTA, just as Mexican goods fall in price in U.S. markets, so are U.S. goods lower priced in Mexican markets. The elimination of Mexican tariffs on U.S. goods but not Canadian goods in a MUFTA leads to trade diversion losses for Canada in Mexican markets. Although present Canadian exports to Mexico are not large, the gain in preference for U.S. firms is large because of the greater Mexican tariffs. Thus, Canadian firms lose a significant share of their present market in Mexico. I have estimated this loss to be $21 million worth of exports.

NAFTA

Under a NAFTA, Canadian exports to Mexico do not fall due to trade diversion since both Canadian and U.S. prices fall by the same amount (the equivalent reduction in tariffs for both countries). Thus table 3 has a zero here.

Static Trade Creation Gains—Canadian Producers-Mexican Market

MUFTA

Under a MUFTA, the U.S. gains preferential access to Mexican markets; Canada loses sales to the U.S. and gains no sales, either at the expense of domestic Mexican producers or at the expense of producers/exporters in countries outside North America. Hence, a zero in table 3.

NAFTA

When Canada is included in a NAFTA, Canadian prices fall in Mexico, not relative to U.S. producers (since both receive equal tariff reductions), but relative to two groups of producers—domestic Mexican producers and producers/exporters outside the U.S. and Canada who now face increased competitive pressure from Canadian imports to Mexico. Thus, Canadian exporters in a NAFTA gain doubly in Mexican markets. The gain in exports at the expense of Mexican domestic producers is labelled as "direct" and comes to some $93 million. The gain at the expense of third country exporters is labelled as "indirect" and comes to $76 million. As the Mexican economy and imports boom, this preferential access for Canadian exporters could be very valuable (the "Growth Dividend" discussed below).

Production Losses—Canadian Market

MUFTA

A Mexico-U.S. free trade agreement provides Mexican producers with increased access to Canadian markets. This assertion appears odd, since a Mexico-U.S. trade pact that excludes Canada does not reduce tariffs for Mexican producers in Canadian markets. However, two effects do increase penetration of Mexican goods in Canadian markets even when Canada is not part of the deal. First, Canada and the U.S. have a free trade pact with certain rules of origin defining what goods are of "CAFTA content." A MUFTA will lead to increased Mexican components in U.S. goods. If this increased Mexican value-added still leaves the final good as a "CAFTA" good, then it can be imported into Canada duty free. Second, as noted earlier, Mexican firms will gain specialization and scale economies as a result of their increased penetration of U.S. markets. These gains in economies and the ensuing productivity gains and cost and price reductions will make Mexican goods more formidable competitors in Canadian markets. Thus, a MUFTA, an agreement which does not directly involve Canada, will lead to an increased penetration of Mexican goods into Canadian markets. There is no estimate of the amount of Mexican gains and thus Canadian losses, so table 3 has a minus sign here.

NAFTA

Directly including Canada in a trade agreement with Mexico means eliminating tariffs on Mexican imports into Canada. However, this is different in degree only from what will happen in a MUFTA (or what is happening now).

Mexican exports to Canada will increase in a NAFTA, some of this increase coming at the expense of domestic Canadian producers. I have estimated this production loss for Canadian producers to be some $125 million (Waverman, 1990). This estimate is based on extrapolating past behaviour and could be an underestimate. This increased access for Mexican goods is the fear that Canadians have of a NAFTA, i.e., of competing with low-wage Mexican labour. I discuss the issue of low wages in more detail below. Another important issue for Canada is the impact of these new trade pacts on longer-term investment prospects. Investment in Canada is a function of the rate of return to be earned on that investment. Two sources of funds for investment in Canada are the domestic and foreign savings pools. One must be careful to distinguish between real investment—the placement of new longer-term productive assets—and savings—the pool of resources available for investment.

Investment is put in place when the expected rate of return exceeds the cost of capital (the cost of capital includes risk factors). Investment in the Mexican economy has been limited largely to the domestic Mexican savings pool since Mexico put severe constraints on the ability of foreigners to acquire or build productive assets in Mexico. In addition, the required rate of return on Mexican real investment by foreigners was likely high since there was a larger risk element for the perceived uncertainty of the economic and political regimes. By liberalizing foreign investment rules and by codifying these rules in state-to-state treaties such as a trade pact, foreign investment will flow to Mexico in increasing quantities (as Ramirez's paper shows).

The world savings pool is huge and even an increase in FDI in one country of $10 or $20 billion per year is not at the expense of any other particular country. The world pool of savings is invested in a wide range of securities—FDI, government bonds, etc., and this pool of savings is not fixed, instead the amount the savings rise reflects the amount earned on savings—interest rates. Thus, if the FDI in Mexico in the future was incremental to all other FDI, a small increase in world interest rates would add new savings to the world savings pool. Peter Pauly (1990) has estimated that an increase of $20 billion U.S. per year for five years invested in Eastern Europe would raise world interest rates one-half of one percentage point. In other words, increases in investment in Mexico need not crowd out investment in Canada (except so far as the rise in interest rates chokes off some investment).

Canadian concerns over investment diversion thus relate not to overall macro-economic forces but to particular industry specific micro-economic issues. Will auto parts plants or textile plants shift to Mexico from Canada? This micro-economic investment issue has to be examined in two contexts—individual sectors and overall effects on the economy. I begin with the overall effects. Assume that a large Canadian plant producing and exporting widgets to the U.S. shuts down and moves to Mexico. The fall in Canadian exports (due to the plant closure) means in the first instance that there are less

U.S. dollars being offered in exchange for Canadian dollars.[13] This means a greater foreign capital in-flow into Canada must occur since there has been a fall in the Canadian surplus on trade (or an increase in the deficit on current account) or, most likely, the Canadian dollar depreciates. If the Canadian dollar depreciates, then the price of Canadian exports in foreign markets falls and the price of imports into Canada rises, leading to trade adjustments (increased exports, decreased imports) to offset the initial impact of the drop in Canadian exports due to the plant closure. If the foreign capital in-flow increases then the loss in exports will not depreciate the Canadian dollar. However, an increase in the in-flow of foreign capital likely represents investment in Canada, offsetting the plant closure.

I have examined potential investment "diversion" in several specific sectors (principally the automobile industry) elsewhere (Waverman, 1990). There is no doubt that a free trade agreement with Mexico makes that country a more attractive place for future assembly plants. Four points are important to consider. First, it is primarily U.S. involvement in that trade pact which makes Mexico an attractive alternative. Canadian absence from a North American free trade agreement will not deter that investment aimed at more than the Canadian market from considering a Mexican location. Second, a serious examination of the future potential of the Mexican automobile sector sees the possibility of locating there mainly cars and parts presently manufactured and assembled in Asia (Womack et al., 1990). Third, to the extent that out-sourcing to Mexico lowers the costs of production of Canadian industry, then investment (and jobs) are retained in Canada. (For an analysis of such a case examining the impact of maquiladoras in Mexico on U.S. employment see USITC, "The Use and Economic Impacts of TSUS Items 806.30 and 807.00," 1988.)

Finally, the net effect on Canadian production of a NAFTA can be positive, when the potential "growth dividend" is considered. In that case, investment in Canada is encouraged, because of increased access to the Mexican market.

Specialization Gains for Canada

MUFTA

A MUFTA yields specialization gains for Mexico but none for Canada. Since Canada does not increase its trade flows (they are in fact reduced), there are no gains to specialization for Canada under a MUFTA (table 3 has a zero here).

---

13 The example also holds for a plant closure when the plant sells in the domestic Canadian market. When it closes, imports rise and the impacts are as in the rest of the above example.

NAFTA

A NAFTA allows for Canada-Mexico trade, therefore the potential for trade specialization gains exists (table 3 has a plus here).

Terms of Trade Effects

MUFTA

It is unlikely that a MUFTA would alter the relative prices of Canadian exports and imports. The reason is simple: Mexico has too small a share of world markets Canada competes in for changes in the U.S. tariffs facing Mexico to alter the relative prices of Canadian exports (and imports) thus table 3 has a zero here.[14]

NAFTA

Opening the Canadian market to Mexican producers and the Mexican market to Canadian producers will affect domestic prices in each country only in so far as the new imports determine domestic prices. This is unlikely. Thus table 3 has a zero here, the same as under MUFTA.

Impacts on Economies of Scale and Productivity on Canada

As noted earlier, the great proportion of the gains (75 percent and more) estimated to accrue to Canada in a CAFTA were from the capture of economies of scale and ensuing productivity improvements. The increased access to U.S. market plus the specialization gains through trade creation lead to lower costs through higher output per plant. These estimates were not based on conjecture. Globerman (1989) provides an analysis of these types of gains to Canadian manufacturing industry that followed from tariff reductions in the GATT rounds, and they show that the reduction in the Canadian tariff led firms to increase their scale of operation and to lower costs of production.

MUFTA

In a MUFTA, there are no export gains to Canada; instead there are export losses in both the U.S. and Mexican markets. As a result, there can be no economies

---

14 To the extent that Mexican competition does reduce U.S. domestic prices, the terms of trade effects for Canada will be negative (we will need to export more to pay for a given amount of imports). It is possible that increased U.S. competition in Mexican markets will lead to a fall in the prices that Canadian exports receive in Mexico, if so, the terms of trade effects for Canada will be negative. However, the small size of Canadian exports to Mexico makes any effect on the overall terms of trade negligible.

of scale or productivity gains to Canadian producers. Indeed, while the production losses for Canada are relatively small, they would tend to lower the scale of operation in Canada, thus reducing productivity and increasing costs of production in Canada. Table 3 has a negative sign here.

NAFTA

As shown below, in a NAFTA Canadian production increases, thus the potential exists for increased scale economies in Canada. Table 3 has a plus here.

Dynamic Gains

MUFTA

There are no dynamic gains, such as improvements in entrepreneurship or changes in the focus of the economy, for Canada with a MUFTA. Indeed, an implicit or explicit desire by Canadian officials to stay out of a NAFTA would reflect a fear of dynamism and change. Table 3 has a zero here.

NAFTA

As I have shown, Mexico represents an opportunity and a challenge. Accepting this indicates a dynamism on the part of Canada. The opportunity and ability to restructure the Mexican economy is exactly the entrepreneurial ability that Canadian business could focus on. Table 3 has a "plus" here.

The Growth Dividend

In the previous chapter, Rogelio Ramirez de la O estimates the changes in Mexican GDP, investment, in-flow of capital, and current account balances following a free trade agreement. He shows that the expected growth in Mexico following a free trade agreement leads to large current account deficits for Mexico. Both exports and imports increase enormously, particularly imports. Actual imports in 1990 were $28.5 billion; Ramierez's estimates for 1995 have imports at $84.4 billion, nearly a three-fold increase in five years. This pattern of imports increasing faster than exports is common to the experience of developing countries which have open borders.[15] As a corollary to the import boom, there is also rapid growth in foreign investment.[16] The import surge reflects the demand for capital goods and technology to build new industrial

---

15 For example, Spain's imports grew at an annual rate of less than 1 percent between 1980 and 1986 and at a rate near 15 percent between 1986 and 1989.

16 The stock of FDI in Spain increased five-fold between 1985 and 1988 (from $10 billion U.S. to $49.67 billion, see IMF, International Financial Statistics).

capacity. Mexican infrastructure (communications, transportation, industry) is not at the level of that in Canada and the U.S. Therefore, the demand for investment and capital goods will surge in Mexico.

Where Canada is not included in a trade pact, this surge in Mexican demand will be filled by U.S. firms—the only firms with preferences (trade and investment) in the Mexican market.

A rough calculation of the magnitude of the potential "growth dividend" for Canada is as follows. Canada presently fills 3.3 percent of Mexican import demand. As I showed above, this Canadian share falls in a MUFTA because of the advantages to U.S. firms and rises in a NAFTA because of advantages over non-North American firms.

Using values for the incremental Mexican current account deficit (the excess of imports over exports) due to the trade pact corresponding closely to those estimated by Ramirez provides the following estimate:

Mexican net current account deficit above 1990 level

	1991	1992	1993	1994	1995
(U.S. $, billions)	3	9	11	11	11

Under a MUFTA Canadian firms can expect to gain some 2 percent of this incremental demand and therefore enjoy increased net exports of:

	1991	1992	1993	1994	1995
(U.S. $, millions)	60	180	220	220	220

However, under a NAFTA, it is not unreasonable to assume that Canada's share of Mexican trade rises from 4 percent in 1991 to 6 percent[17] in 1995, yielding increased net exports at:

	1991	1992	1993	1994	1995
(U.S. $, millions)	120	400	550	600	650

Thus, the "growth dividend" for Canadian industry from a NAFTA could be large.

Canada has expertise in many areas where Mexico requires substantial upgrading and investment—in telecommunications, transportation, energy and mineral developments, and medium scale industry, among others. Thus, the Mexican market ($84 billion worth of imports in 1995) represents an enormous opportunity for Canada, but only if Canada and Mexico are in the same trade pact.

---

17 This is a conservative assumption. After Spain's entry into the EC, the pattern of its imports shifted markedly towards the EC.

Why Canada May Not Opt for a North American Free Trade Agreement—The Politics of Free Trade

I have demonstrated that a North American free trade agreement is in Canada's economic interests. Based on the data I have used, a U.S.-Mexico free trade agreement could cause small economic losses to Canada, but a NAFTA would bring net economic gains to Canada.

Economic reality is not political reality. There are severe problems in coalescing Canadian opinion and the political agenda to make NAFTA a priority item or even an item on the federal agenda. The salient issues are:

- a lack of political will, federal and provincial;
- macro-economic factors;
- a lack of private interest groups or stakeholders who perceive real gains from NAFTA;
- the existence of a stakeholder who perceives clear losses—organized labour;
- a lack of objective informed media;
- a lack of a Canadian vision of the next century.

Political Difficulties

Canada appears to be degenerating into an ungoverned federal state where regional/cultural/internal factors are taking precedence over most outside concerns, particularly concerns like Mexico which appear distant. It appears to outsiders that the Canadian Department of External Affairs spends more time analyzing Iraq than Mexico, although Canada can do little about the former.

The party in power (Progressive Conservative or PC) has such a low standing in the recent public opinion polls that at one point in the autumn of 1990, the commercial mortgage rate (15 percent) was above that party's popularity (14 percent). With the parliamentary system, normally one could assume that majority governments, even very unpopular ones, could pass legislation. However, the peculiarities of the structure of Canadian federal governance gives some power (mainly delay) to an appointed (not elected) Senate. That Senate, dominated by the Liberal party until a constitutional ploy by the PCs temporarily increased the size of the Senate by adding eight new PC appointees, has been vociferous in opposing the imposition of a federal value-added tax (the General Sales Tax or GST). The animosity created by these partisan politics is quite unique and frightening.[18] Thus, the PCs face a battle-

18 Most economists agree with the GST.

hardened Senate which will become (once the temporary appointees leave) a Liberal stronghold ready to wage war again. The Liberals were and are opposed to CAFTA; the Liberal leader has declared that if elected he would tear up the agreement. A NAFTA faces a rough political ride.

Troubling as these issues are, they are moot compared to the internal divisions arising within Canada. These divisions are not new, but have tended to remain below the surface. What is new is that for the first time, *all* these divisions are pressing for power, at levels not seen before and with a paralysed, unpopular federal government which has lost its unique base. That unique base was Quebec. The PCs enjoyed enormous success within that province, and Quebecois held a large proportion of cabinet positions (37 percent in 1989 versus 25.5 percent of the population). But the failure of the most recent attempt to bring Quebec into the 1982 Constitution of Canada (the "Meech Lake" Accord, a "unanimous" 1987 agreement that had to have been ratified by each province by June 30, 1990) ended in disaster. Thus, Quebec is redefining its role in Canada. Unlike the late 1970s when Quebec sovereignty was opposed by Quebec business leaders and academics, now explicit and tacit support for some form of sovereignty by most francophone stakeholders is evident. The issue of Quebec is so crucial to the country and the PC federal government that Mexico becomes a distant, unimportant issue.

Disenchantment is not unique to Quebec. Canada is a long, thin thread of population without the assimilation properties of the U.S. melting pot. The western provinces are far from Ottawa and have had severe acrimonious fights with the federal government (but not the PCs) over resource policies. It is a generalization to argue that the western provinces are aggrieved by the francophone demands on the federal government but the West is growing disenchanted with rule by Ottawa. The middle of the country is not safe territory either. In September 1990 the New Democratic Party (a Canadian version of European Social Democrats) swept to power for the first time in Ontario, the populous, rich, manufacturing heartland of Canada; that NDP government has strong ties to organized labour and is opposed to CAFTA.

Quebec would likely support a NAFTA (Quebec was a strong supporter of CAFTA) but the vision is inward at this point. The West sees no strong gains; Mexico will not import their energy and would be a competitor in petrochemicals. Ontario is now governed by a party strongly opposed to CAFTA. Canada is thus a country staring at its navel; Mexico is not perceived as central to Canada's future. Timing is poor, politically.

Macro-economic Factors and the Lack of Stakeholders

Timing need not be poor if there is some strong stakeholder support for free trade with Mexico. That stakeholder is not apparent. One would think that

Canadian business lobby groups (Canadian Manufacturer's Association, National Council on Business Issues, and others) would be lobbying for free trade with Mexico given their lobbying for free trade with the U.S., and given the realities of the estimates I have made, estimates clear to the business community. Some statements of support have been made but the corridors of Ottawa are not packed with lobbyists fighting for a deal with Mexico.

There are a number of reasons for this seeming disinterest. Paramount is the hyperattention on recent plant closures in Canada, which the media associate with the CAFTA. Macro-economic conditions in Canada are poor at this point, particularly to support the longer term restructuring that CAFTA creates. High nominal and real interest rates, a high Canadian dollar (caused by the high interest rates), and a recession are not conditions that assist investment and long-term restructuring. Given the federal government's surprising reluctance to provide the analyses to disentangle the impacts of macro-economic conditions and CAFTA on plant closures, it would be a foolhardy business group that would lobby publicly for free trade with Mexico. The perception in Canada is that CAFTA has hurt the economy; no-one is busy changing that perception.

If some business group had a lot to gain from Canadian entry into NAFTA then some vocal support would exist. It appears that little Canadian business interest in Mexico exists. There are various reasons for this. First, there are a number of sectors where interest in Mexico is high—telecommunications and automobiles are paramount. But firms in these sectors (that would want an agreement with Mexico) have U.S. plants and thus the marginal benefits to them of a NAFTA over a MUFTA are small. Second, most Canadian industry has no knowledge of Mexico or the opportunities it represents. The gains to Canadian industry from secure access to their already largest market in the face of increasing U.S. protectionism was enough to galvanize their support for a CAFTA. There is nothing about Canada-Mexico trade to galvanize any industry's support. Finally, industries dependent on high labour content face competition from Mexico. Organized labour in Canada is opposed to free trade with Mexico, as it was opposed to free trade with the U.S., but for a different reason—fear of $1.60/hour labour.

Fear of Low Wage Mexican Labour

Opposition to a NAFTA will come from blue-collar unionized and non-unionized labour who feel that they will bear the brunt of increased Mexican competition. And they will. However, the job losses due to increased Mexican competition in Canadian markets are, in my calculations, more than offset by the job gains to Canada due to penetration of Mexican markets.

How can this be so? As we have seen, a MUFTA yields the U.S. advantages over Canada in Mexican markets. A NAFTA eliminates those U.S. advantages.

A NAFTA also yields new advantages for Canadians vis-à-vis Mexican producers plus clear advantages for Canadian producers in growing Mexican markets compared to non-North American producers. In my opinion, the sum of these three advantages in a quickly growing Mexican market more than offsets the job losses in Canada from increased Mexican penetration.

Lipsey and Smith (1985) discuss the fear of competition with low wage labour and provide counter-arguments. First, if Mexican exports penetrate Canadian markets, then the Canadian dollar will fall given the new current account deficit. This fall will boost Canadian exports and reduce imports with Canada. The labour employed in Canada will not be low wage competing with that Mexican comparative advantage but high wage, high productivity labour.

Wages in Canada are much higher than in Mexico because Canadian labour is better-educated, has higher skill levels, works with more capital, and is more productive. Wages in Mexico are low partly because the marginal productivity of labour is low; wages in Canada are high because the productivity of Canadian labour is high.

These economic arguments will be dismissed by labour as the academic musings of an ivory towered and tenured professor. It's fine to talk about the tendency of the exchange rate to equilibrate to shift resources. Two problems exist—the exchange rate does not appear to have done its job in the last year, and shifting resources throws a lot of people with few skills or with industry specific skills out of work. The answer will again appear academic, but is correct. The federal government must clean up its economic mess, reduce its deficit so that interest rates and the exchange rate can fall. In addition, the government must restructure adjustment programs to accommodate the increasing diversity of skills required by shifting trade patterns. Canada cannot afford to forego restructuring. Instead of fighting industry reorganization, Canada must establish a climate amicable for restructuring.

What if I am wrong? What if I have underestimated the ability of Mexican producers to lower costs and penetrate markets? In 1970 I would not have forecast the enormous gains that Japanese producers have made in Canadian markets. First of all, these gains are also direct gains to Canadian consumers who receive the advantages of lower prices, greater variety and choices, and higher quality. In most public analyses of gains and losses from trade, the attention is too often concentrated (as I have) on job gains and job losses. Yet, even with the enormous Japanese penetration of the Canadian and U.S. markets since 1970, the Canadian economy has created 4.6 million jobs. We do adjust to new competitive pressures.

Media

The media in Canada are no help for a NAFTA. Though there are exceptions, most are ill-informed about economics in general, and about trade and Mexico in particular. Articles and programs concentrate on the plants that have moved in the last year to Mexico. The media never report a very large number of these plants, nor do they examine the plants that have indirectly moved to Taiwan, with whom Canada is not contemplating a trade pact. The media generally are not a source of support for NAFTA.

Summary and Conclusions: A Canadian Vision of North America

What is missing from the previous section is a vision of where Canada should be heading. Let me indicate why a NAFTA is of assistance in establishing that vision.

In 1989 a minimal relationship existed between Canada and Mexico—trade flows were low ($2.7 billion in total); foreign direct investment was minimal; few real issues galvanized these two countries to seek common aims and common policies. Yet one real issue has long dominated the economic and political agenda in these two countries—their relationship with the United States.

Canada's relationship with the United States has been of enormous value and importance to the two countries. Canada and the United States share the world's longest undefended border and the world's largest bilateral trade flow. Yet the 1989 Canada-United States Free Trade Agreement came 31 years after the formation of the European Economic Community in 1958 and does not provide the liberalized trade and investment climate that the European Community has enjoyed for at least a decade. When one compares the vision of "Europe 1992" with the current state of Canadian-U.S. integration, a wide gap is obvious.

There are several possible explanations why Canada and the U.S. have not advanced to a common market. One explanation is that the longstanding economic ties between the two countries are so prevalent and obvious that a conscious move to a common market is unnecessary. When one examines the remaining barriers to trade, investment, capital and labour flows in North America, one is struck by their magnitude, not by their absence. The world's longest undefended border has real economic barriers. Therefore, a second explanation holds for the absence of a common market—the persistent and obvious Canadian ambivalence to the U.S.

A Mexico-Canada-United States free trade agreement is an important political step towards introducing hemispheric free trade, the multilateral conditions which will deter Canadian ambivalence towards a common market;

that common market will be broader than the two most northern countries of the Americas.

The pace of recent economic and political developments in the European Community is surprising to North Americans. The ability of the two Germanies to re-unify rapidly with the acceptance of re-unification by European neighbours is astonishing. However, it is likely that without the European Community such acceptance would not have occurred. Europe can withstand the increased economic and political power of a united Germany precisely because there is a Community, a set of legal, economic, and political principles and rules that bind the unilateral exercise of German power. Canadians fear Americans partly because there is not such a similar set of binding rules and institutions in North America. Canadians fear their loss of sovereignty in a free trade agreement or its evolution to a customs union and a common market. But, the Canadian loss of sovereignty is more than offset by a much larger loss of sovereignty for the U.S. Sovereignty is a function of the ability to act unilaterally; common North American rules and institutions can greatly limit U.S. sovereignty (the sovereignty to hurt its neighbours).

North America requires multilateral negotiations that pave the way to a common market. With a common market, the U.S., Canada, and Mexico will cede sovereignty to North American community institutions and laws, and this is when the U.S. will lose its power to unilaterally harm its neighbours. Canada should welcome that loss in U.S. sovereignty (and in Canadian sovereignty) for then cultural, national, social, regional, and local differences can flourish.

Besides the political benefits of a North America free trade agreement, there are clear economic benefits to Canada. A Mexico-U.S. free trade agreement leaves Canadian firms and investors at a competitive disadvantage as compared to their U.S. competitors in Mexican markets. With the expected growth in Mexican incomes and surges in import and foreign investment demand, this competitive disadvantage of Canadians will minimize their access to this larger and growing market.

Any losses to Canadian firms in U.S. markets (and there will be losses) due to increased access of Mexican firms is a cost to Canada, but a cost which is levied equally in a Mexico-U.S. trade pact. Whatever trade is diverted from Canadian exporters to Mexican exporters in U.S. markets will occur whether Canada is in or out of the agreement.

Staying out of trade agreements with Mexico does not limit Mexican penetration of domestic Canadian markets. Canada does not have trade pacts with Japan, Korea, Taiwan, Singapore, Hong Kong—all countries that have made enormous gains in penetrating Canadian markets. A Mexico-U.S. agreement will strengthen Mexican firms so that they will increasingly penetrate Canadian markets. Canadian entry into the trade pact will accelerate this process of Mexican market penetration but not enormously. Mexico will become a more formidable competitor, as others have.

Whether or not Canada joins in a NAFTA with the U.S. and Mexico, Canada is affected in the Canadian market, the U.S. market, and the Mexican market. As Mexico develops, its market potential is enormous; the only way for Canada to enjoy the "trade creation" effects is to join NAFTA. The numbers I have developed show net gains in Canadian production because of a NAFTA.

Canadian self-interest lies in developing closer economic integration in North America and ultimately within the hemisphere. The success of the "Europe 1992" vision, indeed the success of the 1958 European Economic Community suggests a road to travel down. The ability to take that road is politically and economically easier when we have more than one large companion.

References

Brown, Drusilla K. and Robert M. Stern, "A Modelling Perspective," in Robert M. Stern, Philip H. Tresize, and John Walley, eds., *Perspectives on a U.S.-Canadian Free Trade Agreement*, Ottawa: The Institute for Research on Public Policy, 1987.

Cox, David and Richard G. Harris, "A Quantitative Assessment of the Economic Impact on Canada of Sectoral Free Trade with the United States," *Canadian Journal of Economics*, August 1986.

Cline, William R., *External Adjustment and the World Economy*, Washington, D.C.: Institute for International Economics, 1989.

Globerman, Steven, *Trade Liberalization and Imperfectly Competitive Industries: A Survey of Theory and Evidence*, Ottawa: Economic Council of Canada, 1989.

Harris, Richard G., "Comments on Brown and Stern" in Robert M. Stern et al., *Perspectives on a U.S. Canadian Free Trade Agreement*, Washington, D.C.: Brookings Institute, 1987.

Harris, Richard G. and David Cox, *Trade, Industrial Policy and Canadian Manufacturing*, Toronto: Ontario Economic Council, 1984.

Hart, Michael, "Unfinished Business, The Future on the Table: The Continuing Agenda under the Canada-United States Free Trade Agreement," in Richard G. Dearden, Michael M. Hart, and Debra P. Steger, eds., *Living with Free Trade, Canada, The Free Trade Agreement and the GATT*, Ottawa: I.R.P.P. , 1989.

Hart, Michael, "A Mexico-Canada-United States Free Trade Agreement: The Strategic Implications for Canada," mimeo, Ottawa: External Affairs, 1990.

Krugman, Paul and M. Obstfeld, *International Economics*, Glenview, Illinois: Scott, Foresman, 1988.

Lipsey, Richard G. and Murray G. Smith, *Taking the Initiative: Canada's Trade Options in a Turbulent World*, Toronto: C.D. Howe Institute, 1985.

Markusen, James R., "Canadian Gains From Trade in the Presence of Scale Economies and Imperfect Competition," John Whalley and Roderick Hill, eds., *Canada-United States Free Trade*, Vol. 11, Ottawa: Royal Commission on the Economic Union and Development Prospects for Canada, 1985.

Pauly, Peter, "Global Investment in Savings Flows: Some Macroeconomic Scenarios," paper given at a joint Canadian-German symposium entitled

"Developments in Eastern Europe, Savings and Investment Spillovers to North America and the LDCs," held November 1 and 2, 1990.

Rugman, Alan and Alain Verbeke, *United States Trade Actions*, London: Routledge, 1989.

Shiells, Clinton R., "A Disaggregated Empirical Analysis of U.S. Import Demand, 1962-1981," Ph.D. dissertation, Ann Arbor, Michigan: The University of Michigan, 1985.

Waverman, Leonard, "Canada's Role in U.S. Mexico Trade Talks," mimeo, Ottawa: Economic Council of Canada, 1990.

Weintraub, Sidney, *Mexican Trade Policy and the North American Community*, Washington, D.C.: The Center for Strategic and International Studies, Significant Issue Series, Vol. X, No. 14, 1988.

Weintraub, Sidney, "The Impact of the U.S.-Canada Free Trade Agreement on Mexico," paper prepared for the Study Group of the Council on Foreign Relations on "The Future of the U.S.-Canadian Free Trade Agreement," mimeo, New York, 1989.

Wigle, Randall, "General Equilibrium Evaluation of Canada-U.S. Trade Liberalization in a Global Context," *Canadian Journal of Economics*, Vol. 2, Issue 3, 1988.

Womack, James P., Daniel T. Jones, and Daniel Roos, *The Machine That Changed the World*, New York: Rawson Associates Limited, 1990.

Chapter 3

A United States Vision of North American Economic Integration

Clark W. Reynolds

Introduction

The United States has reached a turning point at the end of the twentieth century that is as critical and challenging as the one a hundred years ago. Today, because of increasing integration of the world economy, the Promethean potential of new technologies to deliver sustainable growth with social justice cannot be achieved by the solitary efforts of any single state, however progressive or powerful it may be. "United we stand, divided we fall" is a concept that now transcends borders.

As regional movements are taking place in Europe and Asia to facilitate co-operation in production, marketing, research and development, with political democratization and social pluralism, a new vision of interdependence in the Americas is beginning to emerge. It is increasingly recognized that the achievement of national goals calls for innovative transnational approaches capable of responding to the diverse needs of communities large and small, respectful of race, religion, and ethnic origin, and prepared to overcome disparities in income, productivity, and social welfare through negotiation rather than conflict. The new technologies make such a vision attainable.

This essay asks, in terms of the new paradigm of interdependence and from a U.S. perspective, what are the most appropriate means to maximize the benefits of all parties in North America? What dividends may be realized from increased integration of a continent-wide economy in the nineties? Is it possible to secure growth with equity for Mexico's 85 million people, starting from a per capita income level one-eighth of the U.S. and Canadian averages, with positive increases for the northern partners as well? Are some major regions and social groups likely to lose in the process?

For societies as disparate as those of Mexico and the United States, economic space can be linked successfully only if the economic union allows a reinforcement of each nation's unique character. In addition, unequal power relations make the bargaining difficult. Obviously, the benefits from economic integration must be greater than the costs. Moreover, broad sectors of society must perceive the benefits to be greater than the costs if popular political support for economic union is to emerge. It will be argued that an "integration dividend" from trade and investment with Mexico offers the best hope of growth with equity for all of North America, provided that each of the partners is prepared to make the appropriate economic and social investments and political compromises.

The Timing of North American Integration

The vision of this essay is long-term, looking forward to the next 30 years on the basis of reasonable estimates about the scope for agreement among the three North American partners. Given the unusual disposition to co-operate of each of the administrations currently in power, and the challenges they face in a world of accelerating change, the course of the region into the next century is likely to be set by policy decisions over the next two years. There are moments in history when great opportunities present themselves. For North America this is such a time. This paper shows how sensitive wages, productivity, and income in the United States, Canadian, and Mexican economies are to the speed and scope of trade and investment liberalization. It argues that the size and distribution of benefits within and between the three countries are fundamentally linked to the pace of growth and adjustment in each.

The current U.S. deficit, recession, and recent involvement in the Persian Gulf War have serious implications for North American economic integration which go well beyond the short run. In many respects these problems illustrate the need for an integration process even though they place obstacles in the way of adjustment. The economic downturn of 1990-91 may be different from previous recessions in that it is arguably only in part a "demand recession" (a "Keynesian" shortfall in aggregate demand). Specifically, some experts claim that it is also a "structural recession." A structural recession reflects shortfalls in output and employment caused by changes in the pattern of domestic and foreign competition, technological change, and inappropriate skill endowments of workers, rather than the level of aggregate demand per se.

In the current period, some factories are idle and workers laid off because of structural problems which may be suppressing domestic investment, while other weaknesses in the economy are due to macro-economic policies designed to reduce the fiscal deficit and tight credit markets which have a cumulative impact on expectations and aggregate demand. Recovery from a structural recession calls for policies that favour a revival of expectations generated by the prospects of improved productivity and higher returns to domestic investment. In this regard, the scope for restructuring provided by North American integration offers considerable potential for U.S. and Canadian production, since they are complementary to Mexico's needs for producer goods, technology, and intermediate goods and services.

The phenomenon of structural recession has become familiar to many developing countries in the face of greatly increased global competition. Mexico, for example, was forced by the debt crisis of the 1980s to eliminate its fiscal deficits, reduce consumption, and restructure its economy in order to overcome stagflation and restore growth. No longer able to count on foreign borrowing or forced savings, and with its burden of debt only partly relieved by negotiation, Mexico had to rely on its own resources to restructure production away from highly protected import substituting industries to those better able to compete in the global market. Both macro-economic adjustment and industrial restructuring led to an unprecedented eight years of recession in the eighties. For the United States, the process of industrial restructuring began slowly in the late seventies, at the same time as monetary policy was being tightened to fight incipient inflationary pressures. The ensuing high interest rates led to a major recession at the beginning of the eighties. Thereafter, the economy rebounded under the stimulus of defence spending and a consumption boom, fed by tax cuts, easier credit, and the expenditure of capital gains. Though the era of "bipartisan Keynesianism" led to unprecedented fiscal deficits, debt-financed increases in aggregate demand helped to balance the negative (structural) impact of job losses and plant closings brought about by import competition.

U.S. trade deficits in the 1980s, rather than serving to weaken the domestic economy, were offset by the sale of American assets to foreign investors and external borrowing. (Since Mexico no longer had access to foreign debt, it was forced to bite the bullet of fiscal adjustment and industrial restructuring much earlier than the U.S. and at a much higher social cost in terms of wages and income foregone.) So responsive was the international financial system to U.S. credit needs, and so desirous were foreign savers to hold U.S. assets, that the dollar actually rose with the balance of trade deficit, turning the U.S. from a major creditor to the world's largest debtor in the course of a decade. Pressures to improve U.S. competitiveness were dampened by the strong dollar until action was finally taken to drive down its value. By the time the dollar eventually declined, the pace of U.S. industrial restructuring, though noticeable, had been seriously set back, while debt-led government entitlements and consumer spending had been allowed to reach levels that would be difficult to reverse without a major recession.

The irony of the early nineties is that the conversion of U.S. manufacturing, which began in earnest in the mid-eighties in response to dollar devaluation, is finally beginning to bear fruit. Exports are expanding and international competitiveness is being restored in many industries. The positive turnaround in productivity of U.S. manufacturing in the last few years is cited in a recent Commerce Department report (NYT, 2-5-91). But even as the negative impact of restructuring is beginning to be overtaken by the positive effects of more competitive investments, the high level of public and private debt in the U.S. imposes a domestic financial restriction on continued industrial restructuring. Moreover, an associated tightening of credit standards by U.S. lending institutions may also be contributing to the current weakness in domestic aggregate demand, including demand for capital goods. Presumably, if the real cost of capital remains relatively high, domestic investment will increase only if expected real rates of return to such investment increase. In this regard, a Mexico-led integration boom can have important positive impacts on investor expectations in the U.S. An export-led recovery, brought about by restructuring of the three economies toward greater competitiveness, would presumably encourage increased investment in the U.S. At the same time, U.S. government deficits would be reduced by a growth in tax revenues associated with an expanding economy. Hence an "exogenous" increase in domestic investment implies no necessary "crowding" problem in the capital markets.

Expectations of free trade could well augment the efficacy of monetary policy as a short-term anti-cyclical measure. There is a good deal of debate surrounding the effectiveness of monetary easing in the United States, given an apparently high demand for liquidity and high real interest rates abroad. Expectations of industrial restructuring associated with expanded investment opportunities could well lengthen the term structure of financial savings, permitting real resources to shift from consumption to medium- and long-term investment, as well as encourage increased in-flows of investment into North America, including the United States.

In short, improved investment prospects associated with North American economic integration will contribute to an invigoration of the structural competitiveness of the U.S. economy, as well as to short-run stimulation of a recession-prone domestic economy. Longer-term increased export sales to Mexico, in particular, will lend additional support to investment demand.

To be sure, opponents of free trade with Mexico will argue that it will only exacerbate current economic difficulties by contributing to even more plant closures, job terminations, and so forth. While the negative impacts of the early stages of restructuring will eventually be offset by the rising productivity of remaining firms and new investors that respond to the opportunities of techno-logical innovation, skill-formation, and learning by doing, the first effect of restructuring is dislocating and potentially costly. However, postponement of partnership with Mexico because of the U.S. recession and fear of competition from lower cost labour and resources has a high opportunity cost. Integration will hasten the end of the structural recession by speeding up the restructuring process. Furthermore, since a way out of demand recession is to improve business confidence and generate higher rates of saving, investment, and employment growth, this will be stimulated by the greater potential for profits from regional integration and the increased competitiveness that integration affords for U.S. goods and service production.

The unsuccessful (to date) conclusion of the GATT Uruguay round of negotiations makes it all the more important to rely on regional agreements as a "second best" approach in the direction of ultimate global liberalization. The U.S. and Mexico have considerable potential for achieving gains from the removal of trade and investment barriers, both real and psychological, some of which are far greater than those between the U.S. and more distant partners. There is a woeful ignorance and prejudice in the U.S. (and other industrial countries) about the potential for Mexican sources of supply and market outlets. This acts as a barrier to gains from exchange, which could be lowered by a formal accord, independent of its specific provisions, and to the relief of uncertainties about the long-term viability of the Mexican economy.

The recent Gulf Crisis underscores the need for greater regional security in terms of the availability of energy resources. While a trinational energy policy still remains hampered by fears of U.S. hegemony (not diminished by the role of oil in the Gulf War), each country's long-term interests reveal a need for some degree of transborder energy integration, in the case of natural gas and electricity between the U.S. and Canada, and in the case of electrical power between the U.S. and the north of Mexico. The potential of hydroelectricity from Quebec alone offers considerable benefits to the U.S. Northeast. The Crisis also illustrates that the cost of maintaining a global Pax Americana, given the limited resources available, requires that each major power focus on the priorities of regional security while pooling resources for the provision of a global security umbrella that can no longer be afforded by individual states. While this need will almost certainly strengthen the role of the United Nations and other international security institutions, it will also call for new attention to the security of sub-regions including those of Europe, Asia, and the Americas. Trade liberalization is seen by U.S. policy-makers as providing scope for increased political stability in the Americas, since it offers the potential for higher standards of living in Mexico and (ultimately) in other Latin American countries.

The prospect of a breakup of Canada's current federal structure may become a matter of concern for regional investors in terms of possible changes in legal and institutional conditions within Canada; however it should present no problems for U.S.-Mexico economic agreements or for the incorporation of Canada into a North American agreement to which Quebec would almost certainly accede. Even with separatism (arguably not the most desirable outcome for the continent as a whole), separate deals with Quebec would still be possible and indeed even relatively easy given the Quebec government's approval in principle of trilateral free trade.

Mexico's growing regional decentralization in terms of both economic and political processes increases rather than decreases the importance of achieving closer North American economic integration. Greater freedom of north/south trade and investment enhance opportunities at the regional level to take advantage of local comparative advantage without having to attain approval of the central government. For purposes of greater political pluralism, democratization, and functional federalism in each of the three countries, greater freedom of North American trade and investment offers considerable benefits.

The present U.S. recession appears to be slowing the growth of maquiladoras in Mexico (the so-called "border industries," though they are located throughout the country). Since such industries are almost completely linked to U.S. demand at present, they are highly vulnerable to its trade cycle. This condition indicates that for such enterprises, gains could be achieved by a more comprehensive integration to markets north and south, making production-sharing between the two countries less dependent on "marginal" conditions in one or the other economy. In addition, integration will further the objective of progressively increasing the domestic value-added of such industries.

Although greater production-sharing and market-sharing increases the cyclical interdependence of the three economies, it also provides a cushion from cycles generated in the home market, as was the case in the non-maquila auto sector of Mexico, which was able to shift sales to the U.S. market during the 1980s recession in Mexico. And to the extent that North American integration increases the competitiveness of production in the three countries, there is greater scope for escaping from regional trade cycles by shifting sales to other regions.

It is important to note that in some respects Mexico begins the nineties in a stronger economic policy position than its neighbours. It has already paid the price of a drastic decline in real wages and incomes as a result of adjustments in the eighties, and by now circumstances for many are beginning to improve. However, most Mexicans have still to recover the living levels of 1980. The negative impact of delayed restructuring and demand recession in the U.S. on its own population (in the nineties) is likely to be much less severe than the 1980s adjustment was for Mexicans, especially in terms of real wages. But if recent trends persist, the U.S. may anticipate even higher levels of unemployment as well as acceleration in the shift of jobs from higher-wage manufacturing and permanent positions to lower-wage service occupations and temporary employment, with a further reduction in fringe benefits and job security.

As we have seen, the current U.S. recession is a reflection of the continuing need for fiscal reform and structural adjustment, and the same holds for Canada. Whatever the decisions about integration with Mexico, politically unpopular measures must be pursued. But Mexico offers its northern neighbours an opportunity to speed up the structural adjustment process, at less cost in the long run and without the sacrifice of macro-economic stability, because it provides a potential "integration dividend" as we shall see below. In this regard it is important to view integration of the three economies not as a zero sum game but as a dynamic process of transformation toward greater region-wide productivity, competitiveness, and accumulation, all of which are essential to the achievement of each country's social and economic objectives. The penalties for failing to act in the collective interest are either self-destructive autarchy (in an increasingly interdependent world market that is shifting toward Europe and Asia) or an unco-ordinated opening to other regions that would entail greater instability, insecurity, and higher transaction costs, as well as vulnerability to more far-sighted development policies abroad. The "hollowing" of American enterprise through such measures could lead ultimately to the sacrifice of competitiveness and market shares, lower wages and profits, and less technological progress, along with the loss of economic and political power.

Lessons from Europe and Japan

U.S. firms must determine the line at which competition with foreign sources should be drawn in terms of stages of value-added. The most extreme case is the "hollow corporation," which locates only its headquarters (and dividend payments) in the U.S. but farms out all stages of production and value-added to offshore suppliers. The other extreme is the fully protected "import-competing industry," which produces at high costs behind protective barriers and charges higher prices than the world market, thereby earning "protection rents." (Sometimes foreign firms will locate within the U.S. to benefit from the non-competitive profits generated by its import barriers and voluntary trade restrictions.) The American consumer pays the cost of such inefficiency, and the U.S. gradually loses its ability to compete abroad, with erosion in the balance of payments and gradual devaluation of the dollar (further increasing the cost to the consumer and to labour by erosion of the purchasing power of U.S. wages).

Decisions on where to draw the line, in terms of offshore accessing of part or all of value-added, is heavily influenced by trade policy (related to the "levelness of the playing field"). As U.S. Department of Commerce trade specialist Ann Hughes commented to the author recently, "A well thought-through trade policy is the best industrial policy." For our major international competitors, philosophical commitments to GATT goals of global economic integration are accompanied by practical measures favouring enhanced regional trade and investment, often at the level of firm and industry.

A joint approach to liberalization is helping to strengthen the markets of Europe and Japan by creating favourable (and realistic) expectations about their own competitiveness and productivity potential. These expectations have a self-fulfilling character, creating incentives for higher levels of investment, savings, and capital in-flows than would occur without regional integration. Moreover, such lessons indicate that a positive North American approach to the liberalization of trade and investment can be of critical importance to this region's ability to benefit from the movement toward global free trade, by responding to, as well as shaping, the dynamics of North American comparative advantage.

For Europe, regional integration is the primary goal for the nineties, as we can clearly see from Europe 1992, German reunification, loans and debt relief for Eastern Europe, and the incorporation of Southern European and North African economies into the European system. In the Pacific, Japanese concessional lending, bank credit, technology transfer, and regional sourcing at rising levels of value-added for Pacific Rim partners have been characterized as pursuit of a "flying geese" model that permits Asian economies to proceed in formation with Japan at the lead.

In both Europe and Asia regional ties have outstripped growing trade and investment linkages with the U.S. and other OECD partners. For Europe and Japan, there is less a balkanization of global production-sharing and market-sharing than a staged process in which regional ties are designed to enhance the power of local players in the global market. (Note that there are many fewer European and Asian ties to complementary economies in Mexico and the rest of Latin America than to low-wage countries in their own regions, except for the sourcing of raw materials and primary products.)

For North America, regional integration in the nineties is a means of enhancing the leadership and market power of Canada, Mexico, and the United States, in the face of the growing challenge from Europe and Asia and given the possibilities of the new technologies. Through integration, the more developed partners (U.S. and Canada and selected industries in Mexico) are able to combine their research and development, product design, just-in-time accessing of intermediate inputs, education and training of labour, quality control, and management techniques with the staged sourcing of value-added components from strategically located markets capable of providing complementary sources of labour, management, and raw materials at competitive, i.e., lower, costs.

With the removal of trade and investment barriers, the U.S. will be able to take advantage of regional proximity, permitting lower transaction costs, scale economies, gains from learning by doing, scope for scale economies from the introduction of new product and process technologies, and a platform from which to penetrate more distant markets. In such a process, benefits from integration will accrue to Mexico as well, by permitting it to move up the value-added ladder, offering the possibility of widening trade and investment linkages among its own sub-regions and with the markets of other economies in Central America, the Caribbean, and South America.

As wage, income, and productivity levels rise in Mexico, its production will shift to ever higher levels of value-added, allowing sourcing from lower-wage markets. The three economies of North America will move forward together, bringing into the integration process a growing number of participants from the Americas and elsewhere. From such a process, the economies of North America and the Western Hemisphere will be in a better position to gain from trade with Europe, Asia, and other regions.

United States-Mexico Trade Prospects

There is considerable scope for gains from trade through integration between the U.S. and Mexican economies, based on past trends and future prospects of both countries (Reynolds and McCleery, 1989). In the 1980s Mexico's export growth was favoured more by U.S. demand growth than by market shares in the economy of its major trading partner. For most products (auto parts being an exception) the potential remains for enormous percentage increases for Mexico in the U.S. market without significantly eroding the share of other regions. On the other hand, in the face of a slowdown in U.S. growth, Mexico is almost certainly going to have to get a significant amount of its trade growth from the U.S. at the expense of competitors such as the Asian NICs.

U.S. exports to Mexico and the rest of Latin America are more intensive in capital and intermediate goods than final goods or raw materials and primary products. These areas of trade suffered the most severe slowdown during the eighties and are likely to pick up the most during the nineties, especially to the extent that Mexico benefits from integration. Hence the U.S. will benefit disproportionately as Mexico's imports recover.

> One remaining bastion of U.S. competitiveness in capital goods, namely Latin America, has been hamstrung by the debt crisis and related cutbacks in investment...recovery in Latin America would have a disproportionately positive impact on U.S. trade in

this vitally important area (Reynolds and McCleery, 1989, p. 119).

For the nineties, U.S. export gains to Mexico and the Americas depend on the removal of obstacles posed by the debt and on new capital flows. For Mexico, this will be facilitated by the profit potential from North American integration. Already in the late 1980s the improvement in the U.S. balance of trade was greater with respect to Mexico and Latin America than with the rest of the world (Reynolds and McCleery, 1989, p. 120). For the nineties, the restoration of a U.S. balance of payments surplus must begin with Mexico and Latin America.

> Reduction in the U.S. deficit rests partially on an increase in exports to Latin America,...linked to and as fragile as the economic recoveries of high-debt countries in Latin America (Ibid., p. 120).

> The two-year swing from a record (Mexican trade) deficit (with the U.S.) of $4.8 billion in 1981 to a record surplus of $7.5 billion in 1983 accounted for about 40 percent of the $30 billion growth in the U.S. trade deficit over the same time period! (Ibid., p. 128).

Mexico's trade with Canada (its third largest export market) grew more than with all the rest of Latin America between 1979 and 1986. For Mexico, its North American connection is more important than ever—the United States is its most significant area of trade growth. The favoured groups of Mexican exports in the recent past (those with both volume and price gains) have been shrimp, beer, polyvinyl chloride, glass and crystal, steel bars and ingots, passenger cars, motors, electrical cables (wiring harnesses), information processing machinery, and other machinery parts (Reynolds and McCleery, 1989, pp. 121ff.). The best prospects for North American trade in the nineties are beer, steel, autos and auto parts (large and growing surpluses for Mexico), and high unit value commodities (minerals and agricultural products) (Ibid. p. 122).

On the import side, Mexico shows "stop and go" characteristics indicating its sensitivity to balance-of-payments constraints and capital in-flows. Mexico badly needs intermediate and capital goods imports in order to recover and restructure along the lines of its dynamic comparative advantage. The windfall oil price dividend since last August has helped here, as we have noted above, even permitting the accumulation of foreign exchange reserves along with growth. If integration brings about, as expected, large capital in-flows and if imports of consumer goods do not swamp the total, then Mexico should be able to sustain a rising rate of growth necessary to permit convergence with its northern neighbours.

Can Mexico compete with other NICs in a "bear" export market if one should emerge during the coming years? The conclusions of two years ago still hold: "for the time being, access to the U.S. market remains the crucial determinant of Mexico's export potential, credit worthiness, and development capability" (Reynolds and McCleery, 1989, p. 128).

The Integration Dividend

What economic gains are likely to arise from North American integration? Conventional trade theory states that the wider the gap between economies resulting from barriers to exchange in goods and factors, the greater the benefits from removal of those barriers. But there is no a priori assurance that the distributional results of integration will be either balanced or equitable within or between countries. This will depend on political, economic, and institutional elements related to the pattern of bargaining power and its evolution over time. The first step is to explore the potential for what may be called an overall "integration dividend" that might result from a U.S.-Mexico free trade agreement, given the present pattern of output, employment, and productivity and their recent trends in both countries—and in particular for their adjacent border regions.

The initial component of the integration dividend results from static adjustments in response to the removal of trade barriers, as initially scarce goods and factors in each country experience a cut in price while the abundant ones gain, and transaction costs are lowered between the two markets. As current endowments of labour, capital, resources, and technology are restructured in response to changes in relative prices, and as consumers benefit from lower cost goods and services, static gains from integration will be achieved by society as a whole. In the case of the European Community, such static gains were estimated to amount to about 5 percent of GNP including scale economies to existing firms through integration (Cecchini Commission report). Similar estimates have been made for the benefits from the Canada-U.S. Free Trade Agreement. Since U.S.-Mexico trade amounts to about $60 billion, and there is considerable scope for scale economies among Mexican producers once they have secured access to the U.S. market, it is reasonable to expect that static gains from integration for all three countries could be from $12 billion to well over that figure when accumulated over the next five to ten years.

The static gains from integration represent the cumulative "one-time permanent benefit" from trade liberalization, including the elimination of tariff and non-tariff barriers, streamlined rules and procedures for trade between the two countries, cost reductions, and scale economies. They do not include the "dynamic" benefits from new investment flows, technology transfers, or increases in the capital stock and pool of skilled labour that might be induced by an FTA. Making rough assumptions that the one-time permanent benefit to Mexico in the first year will not be less than 2 percent of its GDP, or $4 billion, while the absolute gains for the U.S. will be double that amount, the estimated total first year gains amount to $12 billion. Accumulating these gains over time, and allowing for improvements in the efficiency of resource allocation over time, provides an estimated present value of over $20 billion that could reach $100 billion (cumulative for the nineties) which is less than 2 percent of annual GDP in North America at present.

However, given the fact that Mexico's current GDP is only 4 percent of U.S. levels (despite its population being one-third of the U.S. size), such static benefits from integration are modest by regional standards. The North American economy as a whole had a GDP of $6 trillion at the beginning of the nineties, including $500 billion for Canada (exceeding that of the European Community including East Germany). Integration gains of only 5 percent of North American GDP ($300 billion) would exceed Mexico's GDP by half, indicating that present disparities in the regional economy will almost certainly cause even short-term effects of regional free trade to have an overwhelming impact on that country. Its structure of production and employment will be transformed, with major gains in income and productivity that will trigger conditions for even larger dynamic gains from integration. While the initial impact from a free trade agreement is certain to be more modest for the U.S. and Canada, the longer-term potential from continent-wide restructuring could launch North America into a new era of growth.

The "dynamic integration dividend" from North American integration with Mexico is capable of swamping the static gains for all three partners, particularly Mexico. The main reason is that the present productivity gap between the U.S. and Mexico, in terms of GDP (value-added) per worker, is 5 to 1 ($40,000 versus $8,000 per worker in 1990 in current dollars which are worth one-third less than those of 1980, as used in table 1 below). The gap between the highest and lowest regions of Mexico is 3 to 1 ($11,700 for Metropolitan Mexico City, extending into the State of Mexico, compared to $4,014 for the South Pacific region that includes Oaxaca and Chiapas).

The large regional (and sectoral) disparities in output per worker within Mexico offer additional scope for major gains from productivity convergence, through foreign and domestic investment plus a continuing shift in employment from lower to higher productivity occupations, sectors, and regions. But such gains are not automatic, as we shall see below. They require major capital outlays including infrastructure expenditures if upward convergence is to be achieved. And the danger is that asymmetrical development, favouring those areas more accessible to the U.S. (such as the North), could exacerbate already wide regional inequalities as well as social and political problems within

Mexico, just as they have already within the U.S. and Canada. A North American program of integration must be accompanied by regional integration policies in each of the three countries.

Mexico's Labour Absorption Problem and Continental Complementarities

Mexico's employed work force, which is now about one-third of its (young) population, will be rising as a share of the total as the population matures in response to decelerating birth rates and longer life expectancy. Since Mexico still has a very low share of women in its formal labour market by world standards, and many men are employed only during part of the year, one may expect much higher participation rates of both sexes as job opportunities and education levels improve. By the year 2000, the Mexican labour force will reach 35 to 40 million. How realistic is it to expect significant productivity convergence between Mexico and the U.S. by the year 2000 (in terms of average output per worker) if Mexico's work force increases at a rate significantly above total population growth (owing to the earlier demographic explosion)?

If Mexico's output were to grow at an average annual rate of 7 percent through the nineties (a ten-year doubling rate) it would reach $400 billion by the turn of the century. Such a goal, while ambitious, is not impossible given the potential profits from integration. The net increase in capital stock required to accomplish this objective would average $30 billion to $40 billion per year over the course of the decade, rising steadily from between $20 billion and $25 billion at the outset to $40-$55 billion at the end of the period, not including the cost of replacement of depreciating assets or investments in education and training.

Such levels would call for a net in-flow of foreign capital averaging $10 billion to $20 billion annually. Given the relatively small size of the Mexican economy at the outset, this amounts to only one-third of a percent of U.S. and Canadian GDP. If one adds the attractive potential of an integrated North American market to investors in Europe, Japan, and the Asian NICs, the required levels of investment are easily obtainable. The amount of required resource transfers into Mexico are dwarfed by the present U.S. fiscal deficit.[1]

---

1 Since integration with Mexico will raise GDP in both the U.S. and Canada, the net capital flows southward will be more than reimbursed by their own shares of the "integration dividend" from convergence with Mexico. Although an increase in GDP of some $200 billion over the next decade appears somewhat ambitious for Mexico, given its stagnation in the eighties, the figure represents only 3.3 percent of combined U.S.-Canadian GDP growth during the nineties ($600 billion on average per year,

Despite the possibility of accelerated growth for Mexico through integration, given the large supply of labour in Mexico employed at bare subsistence wages and the certain growth of its job force over the coming decade, Mexican labour would not be absorbed fully without some migration at least through the year 2000. Moreover, with increasing economic ties between Mexico and the U.S., a rise in real wages for low-skilled labour north of the border requires a tightening job market in Mexico with rising productivity capable of translating into higher real wages to the south. Slamming the door on Mexican migration would hurt production in the north, employment in the south, real wages in the south, and thereby real wages in the north, by increasing dualism in the binational labour market.

Fortunately, this does not have to happen. There are important complementarities between the demographics of Mexico (with its young population and rising participation rates) and the United States and Canada (with aging populations and the expectation of declining participation rates in coming years). Already the U.S. stands to lose more by closing the door to Mexican immigration than would Mexico, and it stands to gain from a managed immigration policy with Mexico over the next decade, especially in the rising number of "non-tradable" service and other activities that demand lower-skilled labour and which are difficult to mechanize (such as adequate health care for the aged).

The pressure of underemployed labour in Mexico, which will endure for at least another decade, will act on the region-wide economy in ways that must eventually be addressed, notwithstanding the preference of U.S. and Mexican policy-makers to leave migration out of the current free trade negotiating framework. An earlier estimate of the static gains from integration between the U.S. and Mexico, based on a highly aggregative, computable general equilibrium model of the two economies, provided the following results.

Omitting gains from scale economies and greater competitiveness of regional industry, assuming full employment (at initially very unequal wage levels) in both economies, and calculating only the marginal benefits ("efficiency triangles") from integration, the model estimates static gains from free trade between Mexico and the U.S., in the absence of investment liberalization, debt relief, or major new capital in-flows amounting to $5 billion per year for Mexico, against net losses of $2.5 billion for the U.S., leaving a net region-wide gain of $2.5 billion (Reynolds and McCleery, 1989, p. 135).

assuming annual growth of 2 percent) and is less than Japan's growth in the last 20 months.

However, strict enforcement of the U.S. Immigration Reform and Control Act (IRCA, the "Simpson-Rodino" immigration bill) would have a much larger negative impact on the U.S. of minus $10 billion, along with a loss of $3 billion per year for Mexico in jobs and earnings foregone. For the U.S., the benefits from complementarities in labour markets and Mexican immigration are estimated to exceed the short-run (static) gains from trade liberalization. It is not surprising that some regional interests (e.g., California horticulturalists) prefer liberal Mexican worker immigration policies to freer trade if it is posed as an alternative. A balanced approach would be to allow both to coexist, with the wage impact of trade liberalization providing a natural reduction in migratory pressures.

For Mexico, the gains from trade liberalization, while greater than those from immigration, would be significantly mitigated by a combination of freer trade and tighter migration policies. Alternatively, a combination of freer trade, debt relief (and greater capital in-flows to Mexico), and continued modest levels of migration from Mexico to the U.S. would benefit both countries. "[A policy of] tariff reduction and debt relief, in a general equilibrium context, would reduce migration [from Mexico to the U.S.] by almost 1.5 million..." (Reynolds and McCleery, 1989, p. 136). And U.S. Department of Labor projections of U.S. employment demand in the nineties, under any reasonable growth scenario, indicate a significant need for increased immigration, well above the levels that have been experienced from Mexico in recent years. That demand will have to be satisfied whether or not the sourcing is from Mexico.

While freer trade is certain to reduce the supply pressures from Mexico in the labour market, growth of both economies will be consistent with a sustained flow of workers from south to north for some time to come with rising real wages in both markets. (However, U.S. stagnation and the failure to significantly increase Mexico's capacity to absorb labour in its own industries, through export growth and domestic recovery, would lead to a reduction in U.S. wages at low skill levels for poorly educated youth, minorities, and other marginal workers.)

The model (McCleery, 1988; Reynolds and McCleery, 1989) fails to incorporate, however, not only the static gains to both countries (and especially Mexico) from the reduction in non-tariff transborder transaction costs, increasing returns, and increased industrial competition, but more important, the enormous dynamic effects enumerated in the previous section. If one adds these longer-term benefits from the "integration dividend," the potential gains rise into the hundreds of billions of dollars. Yet the model does illustrate the extent to which the U.S. is already receiving benefits from "silent integration" with Mexico through labour migration, especially in such crucial sectors as agriculture, services, and low-skilled manufacturing operations. For the U.S., these benefits are as large as the short-term (static) gains from freer trade. In dynamic terms, freer trade and investment flows between the two countries will provide a much greater increase in gains to both countries (and Canada), while reducing pressures for migration from Mexico through both supply and demand effects resulting from the relative growth of lower-wage employment south of the border.

Given Mexico's continued limitations on foreign borrowing, debt obligations, and fiscal constraints, as well as the need for know-how to penetrate U.S. and foreign markets and access the best technology, the integration dividend cannot be achieved without significant additional reductions in statutory and procedural barriers to foreign direct investment at every level, as well as an open-door policy to entrepreneurship and innovation. This process also calls for a crash program to provide adequate transport and communications facilities, at much higher rates than is now the case, in the form of new and improved roads, railroads, airports, ports, and a much more dynamic and competitive telecommunications system. A massive effort in public and private education is essential, plus incentives for research and development, much greater access to foreign technology (with protection for intellectual property), and the freer immigration of skilled labour and management needed to bring about a transformation in Mexican production and productivity. The implication is that the true "integration dividend" from U.S.-Mexico-Canada free trade will result not from the static reallocation of resources and relative price changes that are certain to occur with greater liberalization but from the dynamic response of new investment, permitting a convergence of the entire region to higher levels of productivity, competitiveness, and technological progress—a convergence that will permit rising rates of savings and investment and a more equitable distribution of the gains from growth.

Will Integration Lead to Convergence or Divergence?

In recent decades the productivity of Mexico's labour (including returns to capital, resources, technology, and entrepreneurship) first rose significantly and then decelerated, leading to virtual stagnation through much of the 1980s. The figures for 1970, 1980, and 1985 are presented in table 1. Earlier rapid growth associated with the post-war "Mexican miracle" had led to convergence between Mexico and the U.S., so that by 1970 the ratio between the two countries had fallen to 5 to 1. From 1970 to 1980, the ratio fell to 4.2 to 1. But from 1980 to 1985, it remained at that level and by 1990 was closer to the 1970 ratio of 5 to 1. Moreover, the denominator is based on estimates of gainfully employed labour rather than the economically active population. Owing to the lacklustre performance of Mexico during most of the eighties, productivity comparisons would be even more dismal by the end of the decade.

Table 1
Gross Domestic Product, Employment, and Output per Worker in
Mexico and the United States

	1970	1980	1985
Mexico			
GDP (billion 1980$)	75.5	145.9	168.7
Employment (million)	12.9	20.3	22.0
Output per worker ($)	5,600	7,193	7,680
United States			
GDP (million 1980$)	2,060	2,680	3,058
Employment (million)	73.0	88.8	95.2
Output per worker ($)	28,208	30,190	32,125
Productivity			
(output per employed worker):			
Mexico/U.S.x100	19.9%	23.8%	23.9%

Author's note: Estimates of output, employment, and total factor productivity by the U.S.-Mexico Project of the Americas Program, Stanford University, based on Department of Commerce figures for the U.S. and INEGI (National Statistical Institute) estimates for Mexico. Valuable assistance has been provided by Dolores Nieto and Matthew Carnes as well as important earlier work by Geoffrey Bannister. Details on methodology and results by region and sector are available from the author. Note that the estimates of Mexican GDP in 1980 dollars (originally estimated in constant pesos) are sensitive to the conversion factors employed. The 1980 totals in the table are based on the initial 1980 peso estimates converted by using World Bank (*World Development Report*, 1982) GNP estimates for that year, based on per capita GNP multiplied by the population estimate for 1980. The World Bank conversion from pesos to dollars is based on estimates of purchasing power rather than a strict exchange rate conversion. Use of the prevailing exchange rate would give a higher Mexican GNP figure for 1980, owing to relative "overvaluation" of the peso in that year resulting from the positive foreign exchange impact of the oil boom and extensive borrowing abroad. During the 1980s, the growth of Mexican gross domestic product (GDP) was greater than the growth of gross national product (GNP) owing to the significant increase in net transfers abroad resulting from debt service payments (as the balance of trade reversed itself from strongly negative to strongly positive). Hence the ratio of Mexican to U.S. GNP is slightly less than the GDP ratio indicated by the above estimates.

The regional differentials are even sharper between the least developed regions of Mexico and the U.S. (see table 2). The narrowest gap in productivity is still between Metropolitan Mexico City and the U.S. rather than in the border region, despite the fact that linkages between the two countries have been most developed between the two border areas (the U.S. southwestern states of California, Arizona, New Mexico, and Texas and the Mexican border states of Baja California Norte, Chihuahua, Coahuila, Nuevo Leon, Sonora, and

Table 2
Regional Disparities in Output per Worker: Mexico and the U.S.
(Gross Regional Product per worker in 1980 U.S. dollars)

	1980	1985
Mexico		
Border Region	$8,331	$8,500
Metropolitan Mexico City	10,255	11,257
Rest of Mexico	5,442	5,800
Total Mexico	7,193	7,680
United States		
Border States	39,231	40,645
Total U.S.	30,190	32,125

Sources: See table 1; details available from author on request.

Tamaulipas). The following table shows estimates of output per worker in 1980 dollars for Mexico's border region (as defined above), Metropolitan Mexico City (including the State of Mexico), and the rest of Mexico.

Distribution of the Integration Dividend

Throughout the post-war period, the gap in productivity narrowed within Mexico, though the 1980s were a time of slight divergence, not only between the U.S. and Mexico but within Mexico as the crisis and subsequent adjustment and restructuring took their toll. In per capita terms, the gaps are even wider, as we have noted above, since Mexico's economically active population is only 30 percent of total population, while in the U.S. the active population is 50 percent of the total. In distributional terms, there is a danger that the dividend from linkages with Mexico could produce greater divergences within both countries if the growth in investment and productivity is not sufficiently rapid. Under conditions of slow convergence, Mexico's large underemployed work force could act as a drag on real wages in both countries, so that the incomes of low-skilled workers in Mexico would lag behind the rate of productivity convergence, as marginal workers are forced to offer their services at bare subsistence levels. This has been the case over the past decade, at least until the last couple of years, owing to the severely low productivity in much of agriculture and urban informal activities, where the bulk of the work force remains employed. Simple general equilibrium models of employment and productivity indicate that if U.S. growth is slow and the adjustment between the two countries is unduly static rather than dynamic, wages of U.S. low-skilled labour will lag with integration (though the income of "yuppies," skilled labour, and property owners will rise). While there is not space within this paper to go into the sectoral details of Mexican employment and productivity in the 1980s (this is the subject of a forthcoming book by the author), suffice it to say that despite the considerable growth of maquiladoras, most job creation in the eighties took place in the low productivity urban service sector at falling real wages (at least until the last couple of years).

With rapid growth of the Mexican economy (which is only possible through opening to the broader North American market and major capital and technology in-flows), and without closing the door on Mexican migration to the U.S. during the duration of the nineties, it is possible to anticipate a convergence in output per worker between the two countries that will translate itself into a rise in Mexican real wages. Moreover, the potential gains to capital in both countries will be impressive. To the extent that workers participate in asset ownership through employee investment programs, pension funds, and the like, the gains from capital ownership will be more widely distributed. That is, workers would be able to participate more effectively in the gains from growth through returns to investment as well as through higher real wages. The results would hold for the U.S. and Canada, as well as Mexico, if pension funds, institutional savings, and even social security revenues were transformed into true capital funds participating in the newly productive investments from North American integration and global trade liberalization. But in neither country are the financial and institutional savings reforms in place to accomplish such results. Capital market reform in both countries is of the greatest importance, so that potential savings captured by financial institutions, pension funds, and social security can be translated into real investment.

There is doubtless a risk that without adequate provision for the translation of potential savings into actual investment, and without sufficient growth in the U.S. and Canada so that both countries can "run fast to stay in the same place or advance slowly" in terms of productivity growth, incorporation of Mexico's large and growing supply of low-wage labour could act as a depressant on real wages in some sectors of the northern economies. This would be particularly true if migration barriers were completely relaxed in the short run, or if the "integration dividend" were restricted to static rather than dynamic gains. Under such circumstances, the fears of a number of critics of integration could be realized, at least in the short run, and the adjustment and dislocation costs could be considerable in both countries.

If much greater attention is not given to Mexico's low productivity agriculture (where most of its rural workers are employed) and to its own urban informal sector, including the mass of urban underemployed, there could be a widening of the productivity and income gap south of the border as well. Hence integration of the U.S. and Mexico requires immediate attention to transform Mexico's rural sector and, for the urban underemployed, to support small- and medium-scale enterprise (including "niche" enterprises capable of competing in the international market), as well as non-agricultural activities in the rural areas and small towns to widen the scope of productivity gains and to slow the rate of excessive migration to major cities. Pollution in the (subsidized) population centres is already having overwhelming detrimental effects on health conditions, longevity, and quality of life.

Summary and Conclusions

Since the present negotiating framework omits discussion of changes in labour migration laws but contemplates continued liberalization of Mexico's investment rules, there is some asymmetry in factor movements that is likely to accompany increased free trade, such that there will be greater scope for capital to move southward than for labour to move north. Hence the dynamics of convergence implicit in the "dynamic integration dividend" will favour investment located in Mexico. For those in the U.S., the question is to what extent the goods and services they provide, their labour and capital (including education and training), are "scarce" or "abundant" vis-à-vis Mexico. Highly educated skilled labour is likely to be even less abundant on a region-wide basis after integration than within the U.S. or Canada today. For Mexico, it will be important to add scarce human capital to its large unskilled labour pool. For the U.S. and Canada, given the large and growing demand for non-tradable services and the high labour content of such activities, continued scope for immigration of Mexico's abundant and low-cost labour will be important to region-wide sharing of the benefits from growth.

The strategies pursued for negotiation of liberalization call for a trinational mechanism rather than a series of bilateral arrangements called the "hub-and-spoke" model by Wonnacott. Still, as that author admits, there are important asymmetries in the Mexican and Canadian treatment of major activities in the economy, such as ownership of energy and other natural resources (which in the present Mexican Constitution are reserved for nationals), access to agricultural land and coastal properties (also restricted by the Mexican Constitution), and social programs, including public health and entitlements. Hence it is unlikely that any trilateral agreement reached will ensure full integration of all areas of the economy or harmonization of all aspects of public policy. Nevertheless, an "FTA approach" to North American integration is essential, since the continent represents a contiguous geographic region in which the greatest gains, as we have seen, will come from the dynamics of full exchange rather than from piecework bilateralism and sectoral pacts. Once this first step is taken, it is to be expected that the North American economies integrated in an FTA will become a new "hub" in an evolving set of agreements in the Americas, until they eventually produce a hemispheric free trade area. Such developments are entirely consistent with the GATT objectives of global free trade and represent a step in that direction.

In the short run, however, there is bound to be the appearance of some trade diversion (and investment diversion) from a North American FTA. This will be in part a movement toward greater liberalization, since some of the partnerships between the U.S. and, e.g., the Asian NICs have been due to the excessive discounts for political and economic risk of possible linkages closer to home, including those with Mexico. To the extent that an FTA reduces such risk discounts and opens the eyes of investors to the opportunities at hand, the result will be trade and investment creation and not trade diversion. Some U.S. market shares, on the margin, may well shift from Asian and European to North American (and particularly Mexican and Canadian) sources. However, if the results are attributable to liberalization of a regional market that was subject to even greater repression before the FTA than was true for more distant partners, this cannot truly be considered trade diversion Moreover, it is to be expected that the North American FTA will provide much greater opportunities (subject to careful application of rules of origin) for investors from outside the region, as well as linkages between Europe and Asia and the widened North American market.

One area of considerable potential sensitivity is the threat of U.S. imposition of "political linkages" on trade negotiations with Mexico, or of a revival of Mexican nationalism and xenophobia as a pretext for the slowing of negotiations from that side of the border. In both cases, we have already seen efforts of this kind. Mexico is undergoing both political democratization and economic liberalization, and the pace of one or the other is not satisfactory to all observers either at home or abroad. It is a complex system of economies and societies distinct from the rest of North America—with a proud history of independent development notwithstanding its enormous social and economic inequalities. The problems of its internal political-economic integration, along with growing regionalism and fiscal federalism, are perhaps even more complex than those involving relations with its northern neighbours. After a major crisis of unbalanced budgets and state economic intervention, Mexico has finally achieved an impressive degree of macro-economic stability. As its markets are opened to foreign competition, the political system is under pressure to liberalize as well. A paradox results: economic policy reform restores stability of expectations about the rules of the game, but political reform raises questions about who will govern in the years ahead. Closer ties to the U.S. permit political democratization to occur within the framework of a more stable continent-wide relationship, so that economic and political reforms can both take place consistent with a major new phase of investment and growth.

Due to the lack of in-depth knowledge of its "distant neighbour" north of the border, Mexico's vision of the U.S. and Canada is only beginning to improve. There are dark historical memories of economic exploitation and the loss of territory by force of arms. Until recently, prejudices have tended to triumph over informed judgement to the detriment of all partners. Yet the forces of "silent integration" have pushed the economies of Mexico and the United States increasingly together just as they have done with Canada and the United States. Ties are being built in all directions—investment, trade, migration, technology, and tastes—indicating the enormous gains from economic interdependence. What is needed is a more formal approach that permits integration to take place within a legal and institutional framework capable of protecting the interests of all three countries, respecting the differences of their unique cultures and supporting their highest values. For such a mechanism, agreement is by no means necessary on many underlying principles. What is needed is simply the assurance that the integration mechanism can further the scope of each partner to achieve its own goals, working out its own salvation without fear. This is a North American reflection of a global trend, since the pattern of international economic integration is taking on an increasingly regional character. The recent GATT experiences, combined with the momentum of Europe 1992 and Japan's growing links with its Asian partners, indicate that even when global liberalization remains the ultimate objective, regionalism offers a practical step to the lowering of barriers in the direction of eventual globalism.

References

Arndt, Sven, Bela Balassa, et al., "Comparative Advantage in North America: Theory and Policy," Special Issue, *North American Review of Economics and Finance,* Vol. 1, No. 2, Connecticut and England: JAI Press, Fall 1990.

Cecchini, Paolo, *The European Challenge 1992,* U.K.: Wildwood House, 1988.

McCleery, Robert K., "U.S.-Mexican Economic Linkages: A General Equilibrium Model of Migration, Trade, and Capital Flows," Ph.D. Dissertation, Department of Economics, Stanford University, 1988.

Morici, Peter, ed., *Making Free Trade Work: The Canada-U.S. Agreement,* New York: Council on Foreign Relations, 1990.

Reynolds, Clark W. and Robert K. McCleery, "The U.S.-Mexican Trade Relationship: Past, Present, and Future," in Randall B. Purcell, ed., *The Newly Industrializing Countries in the World Economy—Challenges for U.S. Policy,* Boulder and London: Curry Foundation, Lynne Reinner Publishers, Inc., 1989, pp. 115-58.

Reynolds, Clark W., Leonard Waverman, and Gerardo Bueno, eds., *The Dynamics of North American Trade and Investment: Canada, Mexico, and the United States,* Stanford, Calif.: Stanford University Press, 1991.

Schott, Jeffrey J., Gary C. Hufbauer, and Lee L. Remick, "Annotated Agenda: Prospects for Freer Trade in North America," (draft for discussion, Institute for International Economics, Washington, D.C.), November 1990.

Weintraub, Sidney, *A Marriage of Convenience: Relations Between Mexico and the United States,* New York: Oxford University Press, 1990.

Wonnacott, Ronald J., "U.S. Hub-and-Spoke Bilaterals and the Multilateral Trading System," *Commentary,* No. 23, Toronto: C.D. Howe Institute, October, 1990.

Chapter 4

The Case For Trilateralism

Richard Lipsey

This chapter is about a trilateral arrangement between Canada, Mexico and the U.S. My thesis is that any bilateral or trilateral agreement cannot be looked at in isolation; it is negotiated in a context, and, when completed, it is set into a context. In the Canada-Mexico-U.S. case, the contexts are particularly important and to ignore them is to risk seriously misjudging the significance of the proposed agreements. For this reason, I first discuss the broad context in terms of the developing global economy, and the stresses this development is putting on the system governing international flows of trade and investment. I then discuss regionalism and multilateralism in the context of the Western Hemisphere and place the possible bilateral or trilateral agreements involving Mexico into that context. Then I consider both a bilateral and a trilateral agreement in the context set by the previous two sections. Finally, I consider the possibility that any regional free trade agreement involving Canada, Mexico, and the U.S. might evolve into a more comprehensive arrangement such as a customs union or common market.

Factors Promoting Closer International Economic Integration

To gain some insight into the issues these negotiations will raise, either now or at some future date, we need to understand a bit about the developments in the world economy and the institutions that seek to set the rules governing its international aspects.

Globalization

The technological revolution that has occurred in the last 10-20 years has led to a series of changes that are summarized by the term globalization. This process is occurring in almost all aspects of the economy; of particular interest for the present discussion is the globalization of both production and competition.

No longer are national markets separated from each other by high transport costs and producers' ignorance of foreign market opportunities. Today, firms in many industries face competition from firms located all over the world. This competition has given rise to new and growing opportunities for international trade.

By disintegrating the production process, modern technology has allowed it to be globalized. The component parts of a product are often made in many countries and only assembled in its "country of production." Components that mainly require the input of unskilled labour are increasingly being manufactured in low-wage countries while components that require skilled labour are manufactured in high-wage, high-productivity countries.[1]

These changes, some of the reasons for which are briefly discussed below, are affecting all countries that belong to the international trading system. As technology globalizes the world economy, the benefits from eliminating barriers to the free flows of trade, investment, and even labour are increased. So

---

1   This is an encouraging development for the LDCs that have a better chance of developing comparative advantages in less-skilled niches than in the integrated production of whole commodities. Furthermore, the equalizing of wages will raise theirs. In contrast, unskilled labour in more advanced countries may suffer a relative loss of income, at least in the short term (as it becomes less scarce relative to the demand for it). This fear is behind some of the resistance to trade liberalization among union leaders. Yet in so far as it is a problem, it will occur whatever trade restrictions Canada adopts (within the confines allowed by the GATT). On the one hand, globalization means the erosion of any type of special position that was sheltered from international competition. People who were able to exploit such positions in the past will find their relative incomes falling. On the other hand, globalization has been a potent force behind the rising trend of world real incomes based on increased world specialization, trade, and competition. Preventing these developments from occurring in one country will reduce its average real income. Accepting them means that average incomes will be rising, although the relative positions of different groups will invariably be changing. The possible short-run effects of globalization on unskilled labour in advanced countries also provides a strong argument for educational policies (both formal and on-the-job) designed to raise worker skills to levels fitted for high value-added jobs, which are the only ones that produce high private-sector incomes under competitive conditions.

more countries have more to gain from eliminating international barriers. Furthermore, these gains will not just follow the current patterns of trade and investment flows because globalization is rapidly changing these patterns and creating new opportunities for international specialization, even where none existed in the past.

The Communications Revolution

The last few decades have seen a revolution in communications in which such things as long-distance telephone dialling, fax machines, reliable courier services, satellites, fast travel by jet aircraft, and world-wide computer linkages have vastly increased the speed and reliability of communications, while drastically cutting its costs. More than any other single development, this communications revolution has been responsible for national economies becoming less and less distinct as they become increasingly a part of one globalized economy.

Flexible Manufacturing

The consumers of 1990 have a more developed taste for diversity in goods and services than did the consumers of 1950. The combination of these diverse tastes with computer technology has fuelled the new systems of flexible manufacturing. The volume of output of some single homogeneous product, such as the Model T, is no longer the determinant of production economies in many industries. Now production runs of a specific product line can be short, and each line can be tailored to a specific market, sometimes to individual customers. To cover the costs of such systems, firms still need large total outputs but, the costs of switching from one subline to another being small, the length of the production run of each subline does not matter anything like as much as it once did. Furthermore, the costs of marketing and after-sales servicing can be shared among all the product lines. Now the secret of low unit costs, and hence of industrial efficiency, is *economies of scope*, spreading production over a large number of different but related products, rather than *economies of scale*, producing a large volume of a single homogeneous product.

A Service Economy

The economies of the last decade have increasingly become service economies. If the economies of 1950 were personified by a blue-collar assembly-line worker, the economies of 1990 are characterized by a white-collar worker, operating out of an office and using a computer. Science-based production and the communications revolution have partly contributed to the growth of services by emphasizing the service used as intermediate products in the production of final goods. Rising incomes have increased the demand for services relative to goods in final consumer demands.

The growing importance of services has given new opportunities to trade in services. Computer software is needed to organize the flow of communications, and data processing is needed to analyze it. Computer assisted design can be done anywhere in the world, with the result that R&D can often be separated from production centres. Financial services can now be offered world-wide by a firm located in one country, as can advertising and technical advice. Many of these services are an integral part of globalized competition in the production and sale of goods. As a result, goods production and trade is no longer distinct from services production and trade. New opportunities require new rules to liberalize services trade and to ensure that it is not distorted by excessive government intervention (which is easy to do with many devices that are not ostensibly directed at restricting international trade in services).

Knowledge-based Production

In the new industrial revolution of the late twentieth century, knowledge-intensive, science-based products have become much more important than they were forty years ago. Furthermore, the product cycle—the time between the original introduction of a product and its ousting from the market by a superior product—has shortened dramatically. Also, enormous expenditure is often needed before a single unit of the product is ever tested on consumers, and an increasing proportion of total costs is applied to product development rather than direct production.

An important implication is that innovative activity has become more risky. Compared with 40 years ago, more funds are needed before the market can give any indication of potential success and there has been a shortening of the time available to recoup one's development costs before a superior product comes along.

Globalization of markets is one response to this increased risk. The larger the market size, the larger the number of units over which fixed product-development costs may be spread over the product's (short) lifetime. The development of strategic international partnership arrangements is another way in which R&D costs per unit of output may be reduced.

This is one reason why the option of using tariffs to shelter local production designed to serve the local market alone is sustainable in fewer industries as time passes. More firms find that globalization of production and sales is necessary if they are to remain competitive. This is also one major reason why most LDCs have come to realize that hostility to foreign direct investment is incompatible with satisfactory economic growth in today's world.

Transnational Corporations

The vehicle for accomplishing the globalization of production and competition is the transnational corporation (TNCs which used to be called multinationals).

A high proportion of foreign trade now takes place within individual TNCs, taking the form of the "sale" of a product by one branch of a TNC to another of its branches. The hostility to TNCs found in many LDCs in the 1960s and 1970s has now given way to a welcoming mat as governments realize that no country can expect to play in the game of globalized production and competition if it is unwilling to have many foreign-owned TNCs located within their borders.[2]

Acquired Comparative Advantage

In this new, knowledge-based world of multinational enterprises, many countries' comparative advantages seem to depend more on acquired knowledge and skills than on nature-given endowments. Whenever comparative advantages depend mainly on skills that are acquired by management and labour—and possibly also on human institutions—it no longer seems to be beyond policy control; instead it can be "shaped" by public policy (see Lipsey and Dobson, 1986). Probably, and more importantly, it is also shaped by the decisions of TNCs as to where to locate which activities. This determines to which countries they will transfer technology and in which they will conduct on-the-job education. For these reasons, countries that seriously restrict the flows of capital and goods risk losing comparative advantages suitable to the modern world in so far as these advantages are created by the activities of private-sector producers.

This modern shift of the basis of many comparative advantages from natural to human-created endowments emphasizes the need for enlightened government policy. Such policy is needed; first, to create such things as the human capital, competitive conditions, and investment climate that are suitable to private-sector activities that sustain comparative advantages in high value-added lines of production. Second, international co-ordination is needed to restrain domestic policies with respect to such things as intellectual property rights and the encouragement of innovation, in order to curtail self-defeating "subsidy wars" that seek to transfer comparative advantages from one country to another to the detriment of all.

Investment as a Vehicle for International Competition

Globalized firms selling goods need to be present in many countries, both to produce components and the final goods and to develop competitive strategies suitable for the local conditions in major markets. Globalized firms selling services need to be present in all their markets because a service cannot normally be sold without an establishment from which the service is dispensed.

---

2   For elaboration of this change in viewpoint, see United Nations, 1988.

As a result, competition to sell goods abroad has often given way to competition to secure the favourable locations for investment and R&D activities undertaken by transnational corporations. Over the last decade, international investment flows have been increasing at four times the rate of international trade flows. Another reason why firms wish to develop a presence in each of their major markets is to gain a measure of insulation from growing protectionist pressures and from exchange rate volatility. A firm that has a presence in the U.S., the EC, and Japan can shift its production among these locations and be relatively immune both to alterations in trade barriers in these countries and to alterations in their exchange rates.

The Governing System

As a result of the developments surveyed above, the boundary between trade policy and domestic policy is becoming increasingly blurred in today's world. As the Canadian trade policy expert, Sylvia Ostry, points out, the most contentions issues in the Uruguay round of GATT negotiations were agriculture, services, intellectual property, and investment.

In these areas the trade frictions stem from government regulatory policies that were designed to achieve a range of domestic objectives, both economic and non-economic, with little concern for or recognition of international spillover. Such negotiations are difficult because they touch the exposed nerve of sovereignty, and the entire historical, cultural, and institutional fabric of differing societies (Ostry, 1990, p. 17).

Mrs. Ostry[3] has referred to the resulting frictions as "systems frictions," the point being that different systems of domestic policies used to be accepted as background noise to the international game of competition in selling goods. Today, with services, investment, and other matters looming large, these different systems impinge in major ways on international trading and investment relations. Different systems come into conflict and strong pressures are exerted either to harmonize them or to manage the trade that is affected by them.

These systems frictions have created many new problems for the international trade and investment regime. First, as I discuss below, they have put the main international organization, the GATT, under severe pressure. Second, they have led to new bilateral conflicts as nations, particularly the U.S., seek to remove systems frictions by putting pressure on other countries to harmonize many of their policies with those of the U.S.—policies that used to be thought

3   See her contribution in Smith, 1991.

of as purely domestic in impact. Third, they increase the importance of finding new methods of reducing international frictions—by reforming the GATT and/or by making use of arrangements outside of the GATT.

The GATT

The General Agreement on Tariffs and Trade was created in a world where firms competed internationally, mainly by exporting goods produced within their one country of location. The modern developments described above are threatening the GATT at the very basis of its *raison d' être*:

> ...the GATT was designed to deal with a simpler world in which international trade issues were centred primarily on border measures mainly in the form of tariffs...it should be noted, a serious danger lies in the notion of "blurring boundaries": if it is argued that virtually everything affects "competitiveness," the only practicable solution will be managed trade (Ostry, 1990, p. 77).

It remains to be seen whether the GATT can make the transition from its successful governance of the old multilateral order, based on trade in goods which was inhibited mainly by tariffs and quotas, to being able to govern the new, vastly more complex order, based on trade in services as well as goods and with international investment as much a vehicle of foreign competition as the exchange of goods. It is also an order in which systems frictions are growing, and in which governments do not accept the existing state of comparative advantage as immutable. Instead, governments operate rather loosely formulated, but often quite potent, policies with respect of investment and innovation, which are designed to affect their country's economic growth and its pattern of comparative advantages.

Regional Agreements in General

GATT Article XXIV allows for the formation of regional, tariff-free areas as long as these cover "substantially all" of the trade between the partners. There are five main types of regional economic liberalizing arrangements.

The first is a free trade area which eliminates tariffs among the member states but leaves them free to levy their own individual trade restrictions against other countries. This gives rise to two further requirements. First, there must be customs checks on movements of goods between members to prevent imports coming into the free trade area through the country with the lowest external tariffs (called trade deflection). Second, there must be rules of origin to determine when a good is manufactured within the free trade area, and so permitted to move duty free among the member countries, and when it is manufactured outside of the free trade area, and so subject to duty when moving from one member country to another.

The second is a customs union which not only creates free trade among the member states but also erects a common barrier against goods entering the area from other countries. In principle, a customs union eliminates the need for rules of origin and customs checks on goods moving between members. (In practice, most members wish to continue border surveillance to enforce laws, rules, and regulations relating to such diverse matters as gun control, trade in prohibited substances, and animal diseases.)

The third is a common market which is a customs union with the added provision of the free movement of labour and capital among member countries. In a simple textbook world, a common market creates a single economic unit such as exists within the borders of one country. In practice, because of the enormously complex economic relations existing in today's globalized world, a common market is not a single market since many other laws, rules, and regulations with respect to conditions governing such matters as service establishments, investment locations, mergers, take-overs, and a host of other things, create differences in the competitive conditions ruling in the separate markets of each of the members.

The fourth is a currency union, which is a common market with a single currency. This arrangement forces a harmonization of many macro-economic policies on the member countries.

Finally, a complete economic union is required if, in today's complex economies, truly uniform conditions are to be created in all of the forces that influence competition in the production and sale of goods and services, as well as in the conditions affecting investment. This requires that all laws, rules, and regulations relating to all economic matters be harmonized. Such a harmonized economic union would eliminate systems frictions. It could conceivably be achieved short of a political union, but in the complex world systems frictions can arise from almost any laws and, in practice, a political union might be required to do the job.

Specific Regional Agreements

The world has seen only a few really successful regional agreements in this century. One of the most successful has been the European Community (the EC), which is a common market covering trade in goods. Another is the European Free Trade Area (the EFTA), whose members have a single free trade agreement establishing free trade in goods among themselves, with separate agreements establishing free trade in goods between each member and the EC. The next is the Australia-New Zealand "Closer Economic Relations" which establishes free trade in goods and services between the two countries, as well as dealing with a number of other matters including investment flows. A less embracing agreement is the U.S.-Israel agreement which establishes free trade in goods between the two countries. Finally, and most recently, is the Canada-

U.S. Free Trade Agreement, which is a free trade agreement in goods and many traded services with a number of measures covering non-tariff barriers, investment, the movement of business persons, the containment of future trade restrictions, dispute settlement on trade remedy laws, and a host of other, more detailed, aspects of economic relations between the two countries.

Many other regional agreements have been tried, but no others have met with conspicuous success. The main reason is that most of the others have tried for limited tariff reductions that would not have passed GATT Article XXIV had that been necessary. The major lesson from these experiments is that, to be of significant value, free trade agreements need to accomplish nearly complete elimination of all tariffs and quotas—and these days, as the distinction between goods and services becomes more blurred, they should also cover traded services.

Trade and Investment Liberalization in the Western Hemisphere

Mexico's interest in negotiating a free trade agreement with the United States which blossomed in 1990 is symptomatic of an increased interest in many countries of Latin America in liberalizing both trade and investment flows.

Pressure for Liberalization

Here are some of the major reasons for this increased interest in trade and investment liberalization among many of the countries of Latin America and the Caribbean.

- The older, inward-looking import-substitution policies have been discredited in many countries. Along with the countries of Eastern Europe, many other countries are seeking to allow more market determination in guiding economic affairs. Liberalization of trade and investment flows is a major part of these market-oriented policy packages.
- Many of the countries of Central and South American are beginning to feel left out of the great economic events of the post-Second World War world. In a sense, they feel that history has passed them by, with the Triad countries becoming the location of major economic action.
- The globalizing trends discussed previously have made it clear that countries can no longer "go it alone." Rapid growth requires that a country join the globalized economy which implies adopting a liberal regime with respect to both trade and investment flows.
- When the Canada-U.S. Free Trade Agreement has been in place long enough for its full worth to be obvious to outside observers (but probably still not to its Canadian critics), and if a Mexican free trade agreement should be added to this, the other countries will see this as

an obvious way of getting back into the mainstream of economic events. The dream of hemispheric free trade will be seen as the way of exploiting the vast potential of the Western Hemisphere, and of raising incomes and lowering poverty to levels currently found in the EC.

This broader vision of what may be ahead shows the importance of viewing what happens in the next few years with respect to the current Mexican initiative in the context of longer-term developments. Of course, a single hemispheric free trade area may be a long way away, and it may never come about. The forces identified above, however, suggest that an extension of a Canada-Mexico-U.S. free trade area to include several other countries of Latin America is not at all unlikely.

Observers who know much more about Latin America, tell me that the dream of full hemispheric free trade is, and will remain, only a dream. Possibly. But against their opinions based on detailed knowledge of Latin America, I would observe that no one thought the EC would be extended to include all of free Europe; or that even Turkey would desire admission; or that it would be assumed that once the countries of Eastern Europe had restored the market system, they would also be looking to the EC as their natural economic home. No longer does the dream of free trade from Lisbon to Moscow seem the stuff of fairy tales—still a long shot, and still a long way off, but no longer a mere dream. In 1953, when I was a delegate to the Council of Westminster, which was studying the foundations for the Treaty of Rome, that Pan-European free trade area seemed even more unlikely to us than does hemispheric free trade now seem to contemporary observers.

I would add that, as with Spain, Portugal, Greece, and Turkey, once it becomes obvious that the stronger countries of Latin America are making their free trade area work, the weaker nations will feel increasing isolation and conclude that, whatever their destiny inside the free trade area, it could not be worse that what awaits them if they remain isolated outside of it.

Advantages and Risks to LDCs

The less developed countries obtain many advantages by getting into close economic relations with developed nations. Free trade in goods and services probably does not pose any great threat. Inward-looking, import-replacement methods of growth are generally discredited. Free investment flows offer a technology transfer that creates faster economic growth than can be achieved by creating one's own technology behind closed trade and investment barriers. Most importantly, a regime of liberalized trade and investment flows formalized in a free trade area treaty is an important check on future populist regimes which will promise short-term gains, through such income redistribution polices as lowering profits and raising wages, that will bring long-term losses (as they almost invariably have when they have been tried in such Latin American countries as Mexico and Argentina). Whatever governments may be able to do in principle to encourage growth by positive intervention, the evidence from Latin America and Africa is that the easiest way to eliminate growth prospects is for a government to be interventionist with state-owned production and major redistribution schemes.[4]

No course of action, however, is without risk and each less developed country is taking some risks when it embraces a regime that relies heavily on market determination.

Policies with Respect to Foreign Investment and Innovation

In a world in which comparative advantage is often acquired rather than inherited, and where human capital is often more important than physical capital, there may be room for judicious government intervention to tip the scales in one direction rather than another, so as to start off a positive feedback system based on increasing returns. As positive feedback theory (to say nothing of the theory of chaos) tells us, small perturbations can have enormous effects in the not too far distant future. Furthermore, there is still some uncertainty as to whether ownership of the firms operating within one's boundaries matters. Michael Porter has argued, on the basis of his massive ten country study, that it is important for a country to have some home-owned TNCs operating within its boundaries.[5] On the other hand, as TNCs become more globalized in their locations and ownerships, it is not at all clear what it means to assign a nationality to a TNC. Since economists are not quite sure what is the best policy for countries to follow in such circumstances, there are some risks in signing away all rights to follow any sort of foreign investment policy in the future or in severely constraining the scope of some types of innovation policies.

There can be little doubt that if the choice were either total market determination or the sort of government growth policies followed by Latin American

---

4   This is not to say that there is no room for redistribution policies to remove the worst of the suffering that a market economy can meet out to those who are unfortunate in their initial endowments or unlucky in the decisions that they make. But most interventionist policies have shown that the most powerful way to raise living standards is to generate a rising level of national income, without which there is little to redistribute, while excessive concern with redistributing the income that is currently available can lead to a shrinking of future income.

5   See Porter, 1990. Of course, if locally owned firms are to become TNCs, they must be successful in tough free market competition and not just the dependants of state subsidies.

countries in the past, complete laissez faire would be the better choice by far. But, given the degree of uncertainty about appropriate innovation and foreign investment policy, it would be judicious to retain a certain amount of policy latitude wherever possible.[6]

Tariff versus Non-tariff Barriers

Another risk may arise from trading away tariffs and quotas without an equivalent constraint on non-tariff barriers. Countervailing duties (and, to a lesser extent, anti-dumping duties) are the tool of the stronger partner, while tariffs and quotas are available to all countries. For example, many American trade-policy analysts who are critical of the U.S. use of countervailing duties have urged Canadians to mount countervailing cases against the U.S. to show Americans that they also subsidize. When asked why they do not initiate countervail investigations against obvious U.S. subsidies, Canadian firms often reply that if they did so, the Americans would find some other way to retaliate against them. "Let well enough alone, and accept the U.S. subsidies; to try to 'level up the playing field' by attacking the subsidies, as Americans attack Canadian subsidies, would only make matters worse." Rightly or wrongly, that is the attitude of many Canadian firms—and I have heard no other satisfactory explanation of why Canadians have mounted only one countervailing case against the U.S. in spite of the empirical evidence that the U.S. subsidizes as much, more or less, as Canada. Because non-tariff barriers may be more easily wielded by the economically strong, there is a legitimate worry that the U.S. may evolve higher non-tariff barriers while their lesser free trade area partners are reducing their own tariffs and quotas.

In principle, raising the overall level of U.S. tariffs against a background of constant tariffs in a free trade area partner country is similar to a unilateral reduction of tariffs in the partner country against a background of a given level of U.S. tariffs. We know that a country can gain from unilateral reductions in its tariffs—for example, Mexico appears to have gained from its major unilateral reductions in the latter half of the 1980s. The use of NTBs, however, is not quite the same as a general increase in all rates of tariffs because the trade laws are varied piecemeal. In particular, the trade laws tend to be invoked differentially just when a particular export is succeeding in penetrating the U.S. market. Thus, a stiffening of these laws has effects that differ from an across-the-board

---

6   The value of retaining some policy latitude for an enlightened government must, however, be offset against the possibility that such latitude will be abused to the public detriment by a populist government that goes for short-term gain at the cost of long-term loss.

increase in the level of tariffs. The message that this then gives to the exporter is "don't try to penetrate the U.S. with goods, just move your facility to the U.S. to avoid countervailing and anti-dumping duties."

No one knows how the trading system and the non-tariff barriers to trade will evolve over the next decade or two. It is worth issuing the warning, however, that careful watch must be kept on the rise of NTBs. Some way needs to be found to subject them to international control, without which their unilateral determination will no doubt cause their use to accelerate. Entering into free trade agreements with either the U.S. or (if they were willing) the EC, does carry some degree of risk to the extent that the ability to use the fair trade laws as NTBs is greater in the U.S. and the EC than in other less economically powerful countries. It is a risk worth taking since the alternative of no reduction in barriers is worse. None the less, vigilance is well advised when such serious risks are involved.

Of course, one main message that follows from this discussion is that the world must seek to find ways to control the use of NTBs, especially those that arise from a misuse of the fair trade laws. The U.S. Congress has, however, shown no interest in even discussing this issue internationally. Hence the need for caution.

Regionalism Versus Multilateralism?

Many people have worried that there was a conflict between regional and multilateral trade liberalization. Most economists and policy-makers in advanced countries would undoubtedly prefer multilateral liberalization if they had to make an either-or choice between the two. The reason for pursuing both is that different things are achievable through each route.[7] Some of reasons for being concerned with adding regional arrangements to a multilateral regime are as follows.

- There is concern that the more immediate regional negotiations may deflect resources from multilateral negotiations. This is a concern only when the two overlap significantly. In Canada's case, it did not seem to be a problem, both because there was not too much overlap between the negotiations for the Free Trade Agreement and for the Uruguay round of the GATT, and because the country had sufficient resources to pursue its objectives on both fronts simultaneously. In

---

7 Murray Smith and I have argued this point in detail for the Canada-U.S. Free Trade Agreement compared with the possible outcomes achievable through the GATT. See Lipsey and Smith, 1989.

Mexico's case, this may have been a more serious worry. Some Canadian GATT negotiators reported a serious reduction in the important efforts Mexican officials were offering in the Uruguay round negotiations once the U.S.-Mexican negotiations were announced in mid-1990. Mexico may not have had enough experienced trade experts to be fully involved in preparing for, and in carrying on, both sets of negotiations simultaneously.

- There is concern that the existence of regional groupings will reduce the member countries' commitments to the multilateral system. It can be argued, for example, that if they were fully separate economic units, the members of the EC could not have afforded to take the high-handed line on agriculture that they have been willing to take as a group. Without the EC, and its major extension planned under the Europe-1992 program, the individual European countries would have had such an enormous stake in preserving export markets through multilateral negotiations that the breakdown of the Uruguay round of GATT negotiations would have been unthinkable. It is hard to argue with this contention. It is also hard not to give some weight to its application to the Western Hemisphere. If a free trade area covering Canada, the U.S., and Mexico were to be extended to cover some of the major countries of South America, to say nothing of it growing into a complete hemispheric free trade area, the commitment to make the multilateral system work might be diminished.

- As an extension of the last point, the existence of regional groupings may hasten the breakup of the world into trading blocks which reduce restrictions on trade and investment among their members while increasing restrictions on movements among the groups. The significance of this possibility is difficult to assess. If multilateralism is to become less powerful, then regional groupings are a second line of defence for a liberalizing regime. They are certainly better than a return to the world of the 1920s and 1930s in which each country raised its own barriers against all others. However, if the regional groupings encourage the breakdown of multilateralism, they exact a heavy price.[8]

---

8 This issue is an example of what economists call moral hazard. Fire insurance is a desirable protection against fire losses to individuals but, to the extent that it reduces the incentive to be careful and hence causes more fires, it is costly to the economy as a whole. Similarly, regional groupings are an insurance against the weakening of multilateralism, but may themselves contribute to that weakening.

Although there are real concerns here, it is not inevitable that the existence of a free trade area will weaken the commitment to the multinational trading system. Canada certainly did not weaken its commitment to work for the success of the Uruguay round because of the successful completion of its Free Trade Agreement with the U.S. Indeed, in small countries, such as Canada and Mexico, there is concern about having too many eggs in the single American trading basket. For many reasons, some economic and some political, most Canadians would prefer Canadian trade to be less concentrated on the U.S. than it now is. Since a free trade agreement with the U.S. tends to increase this concentration, it tends, if anything, to strengthen the commitment to the multilateral system which is seen as the main route to reducing excessive dependence on trade with the U.S.

I conclude that hemispheric trade liberalization need not be in conflict with multilateral liberalization, but that it might, to some extent, reduce the commitment to such liberalization (although it might also increase it).

The involvement of Canada and Mexico (and later other countries from the hemisphere) in such movements will be based on many considerations including those that follow.[9]

- More trade and investment liberalization is available through regional negotiations among major trading partners with shared interests than through multilateral negotiations involving over 100 countries.
- Difficult issues causing frictions between a few countries can better be dealt with in the context of regional negotiations than multilateral ones. Also, within the broad context of trade liberalizing negotiations, a full set of compromises covering many specific issues is more likely than when the issues are dealt with one at a time in piecemeal negotiations. (This is the same as the argument that full free trade is easier to negotiate than sectoral free trade.)
- Compared with negotiations among the over 100 members of the GATT, regional negotiations among similar economies may have a better chance of dealing with all of the non-tariff issues raised by the modern economies and not envisioned by the framers of GATT, including the systems frictions discussed earlier. The more that the GATT appears to have difficulty in dealing with these issues multilaterally, the greater the apparent advantage in organizing

---

9   For elaboration of some of these points see Lipsey and Smith, 1989, pp. 318-20.

regional institutions to deal with them, at least as back-up arrangements.

- The rapid globalization of the world economy discussed earlier makes it important to use every avenue for liberalizing trade and investment. This is particularly so for less developed and developing countries that are currently behind in the globally competitive game.
- Regional trade liberalization need not be at the expense of multilateral negotiations although there may be some cost in reducing the pressure to keep up difficult multilateral negotiations (the size of this effect is hard to assess).
- No matter how undesirable it may be, there is some chance that the world may tend to split into regional trading blocks that reduce barriers to trade among their members while increasing barriers to trade between the blocks. In this case small, trade-oriented countries, such as Canada and the Mexico of the 1990s, have little choice but to join a block. For Canada and Mexico, there is only one such block available: if there is to be a Fortress North America, Canada and Mexico had better be within it than isolated outside of it.[10]

The U.S. involvement will be based partially on considerations such as those mentioned above. Much more importantly, however, it will be based on considerations of political economy. The U.S. perceives that it has a major stake in the political stability of the Western Hemisphere. Its past efforts to support friendly governments and unseat those that it regards as unfriendly have not always succeeded, and have often provoked serious anti-American reactions. Hemispheric free trade, by increasing economic growth and well-being, offers the U.S. a chance to achieve, by peaceful economic means, the hemispheric stability that has proved so elusive when pursued by overt or covert politico-military means.

Models for the Evolution of Liberalization

The big difference between the bilateral and trilateral approaches to Mexican free trade come when further countries seek to liberalize their trade. There are several models for this.

---

10 There is unlikely to be a choice between black and white. What may happen is somewhat less restriction on intra-block trade and somewhat more on inter-block trade. Since it is a matter of degree, a slow evolution in one direction or the other is possible, and pressure needs to be applied continuously to encourage multilateralism.

The Hub-and-spoke Model

In the hub-and-spoke model, the U.S. has a separate bilateral free-trade agreement with each of the other participating countries. If the U.S. and Mexico negotiate a bilateral agreement, hemispheric trade liberalization will be evolving towards the model of the U.S. as the hub and the other countries as the spokes.

There are several reasons why the adoption of the hub-and-spoke model should be resisted by countries other than the U.S.:

- As the hub country, the U.S. becomes the only country with tariff-free access to the markets of all participating countries. As spoke countries, the other participants—including Canada—have tariff-free access only to the U.S. market. Thus, this model creates trade diversion in each of the markets of the spoke countries; the beneficiary is the U.S. and the losers are the other spoke countries.
- The spoke countries lose from investment diversion to the U.S. Locating a plant in any spoke country provides tariff-free access only to the U.S. and the local spoke market. Locating a plant in the U.S., however, provides tariff-free access to the U.S. and to the markets of all spoke countries.
- The U.S. is placed in a superior bargaining position. It creates separate agreements with each of its smaller partners, so that they have no chance to make common cause against the U.S. in areas of mutual interest. This gives the U.S. a dominance it may not desire, but which the logic of the hub-and-spoke model thrusts onto it. Some Canadians worried that the Canada-U.S. Free Trade Agreement encouraged U.S. dominance in trade and investment. Be that as it may, the evolution of the hub-and-spoke model of regional trade liberalization certainly would have this effect. It is a recipe for U.S. domination of the hemisphere through a series of bilateral, divide-and-conquer deals.

A Series of Overlapping Regional Free Trade Areas

We have already observed that once the success of a Mexican-U.S. free trade agreement (with or without Canada) is demonstrated, other countries will wish to have similar free trade arrangements. Some counties have already expressed an interest in forming some type of free trade area with Mexico. A series of overlapping free trade areas could evolve, with the U.S. and Mexico being inside some and outside others. These would likely have different conditions and different rules of origin. The overlapping mess of conflicting arrangements would cause the types of difficulties and confusions that most people would prefer to avoid. Yet if other Latin American countries correctly come to regard the hub-and-spoke model as not in their interest, this is a not unlikely follow on from a bilateral Mexico-U.S. free trade agreement—unless some superior model of evolution has been made available.

Plurilateral Regionalism

The superior model is what I have elsewhere called plurilateral regionalism (see Lipsey, 1990). I use the term to refer to regional free trade areas (or customs unions, or common markets) in which all members have the same privileges and obligations. In particular, each country has tariff-free access to all other members' markets. This makes the regional grouping plurilateral in the sense that all participants are treated equally, in contrast to the hub-and-spoke model which gives the hub country a position superior to those of the spoke countries.[11]

In the present case, plurilateral regionalism calls for a trilateral agreement covering Canada, the U.S., and Mexico. It is not a matter of the three countries sitting down at one bargaining table to work out separate bilateral agreements with each other. Instead, a single trilateral agreement would be negotiated. Such an agreement would be capable of expanding to other countries in the Americas until it became a single hemispheric free trade area in which all countries of the Western Hemisphere have tariff-free access to each other's markets.

Whereas the hub-and-spoke model is a model of American hegemony over the Americas with each country tied only to the U.S., plurilateral regionalism is a model of equals. All members have access to each other's markets, all bargain together, and all are free to make common cause with others of like mind in common trade negotiations.

If the U.S.-Mexican negotiations are kept bilateral, hemispheric trade liberalization will be moving toward the hub-and-spoke model, with the U.S. already as hub to two North American spokes, Canada and Mexico (plus a third trans-oceanic spoke of Israel). If the negotiations become trilateral, plurilateral regionalism will have been significantly enhanced. The tripartite Canada-Mexican-U.S. free trade agreement would become the agreement to which further countries could accede, creating a growing hemispheric free trade area.[12]

11   I follow usual practice in reserving multilateral to refer to very broad groups of nations and plurilateral to refer to smaller groups. There is, of course, no definitive dividing line between the two since the GATT does not include all nations and plurilateral groups could be as small as three countries and as large as all those of the Western Hemisphere.

12   By supporting Canadian participation in the negotiations, the U.S. administration indicated that it prefers the plurilateral regionalist model over the U.S.-dominated trade hub-and-spoke model. It is an irony that many Canadians who opposed the Canada-U.S. Free Trade Agreement on the grounds that it made Canada too

What Kind of an Agreement?

Advantages of a Trilateral Agreement

The case for trilateral agreement can be approached from two different points of view. First, the agreement can be looked at as a short-term end in itself and evaluated in isolation. Second, the already discussed probability that trade liberalization would spread through the hemisphere means that the agreement can be looked at in the longer-term light of an evolving hemispheric trade liberalization.

A Short-term View

The balance of advantages and disadvantages between a bilateral or a trilateral agreement looks somewhat different from the three countries' static points of view. In each case, we can contrast what the country would achieve through a bilateral, Mexico-U.S. agreement and a trilateral agreement that included Canada.

Mexico

Although a bilateral agreement will get most of what Mexico initially wants, a trilateral agreement offers more. Just as with Canada, a bilateral agreement will give Mexico tariff-free access to its largest market. But under a trilateral agreement, Mexico gets the same access as with the bilateral agreement, plus access to the Canadian market and liberalization for Canadian investment in Mexico. This may mean more competition, both among firms selling tariff-free in the Mexican market, and among investors seeking to enter Mexico from the north to exploit Mexican resources.

Depending on the terms actually negotiated, under a bilateral agreement Mexico will get some security of access in terms of limitations on the use of quotas and the national defence excuse for restricting trade, plus some dispute settlement mechanism.[13] But with a trilateral agreement, it is hard to imagine the security of access parts of any agreement being reduced as a result of Canada's inclusion. Indeed, it would seem more likely that Canada's presence

dependant on the U.S. also opposed Canada's inclusions in tripartite negotiations and so supported (against the U.S's stated wishes) the U.S. domination of hemispheric trade liberalization through the hub-and-spoke model.

13 For a full analyses of all the ways in which the Canada-U.S. Free Trade Agreement increased each country's security of access to the other country's market, see Lipsey and York, 1988.

would increase the strength of any clauses meant to enhance security of access. After all, this has been Canada's main objective in negotiating with the U.S., and it is the U.S. that is resisting any reduction of its powers under its trade remedy laws and any weakening of its ability to act unilaterally to restrict access when *it* judges that the access results from "unfair" practices.

The need to enhance security of access may be much more important than is understood in Mexico today. If the free trade agreement succeeds, and new Mexican products begin to penetrate the U.S. market in a big way, U.S. competitors will make increased use of the trade remedy laws in attempts to thwart this access. As Sylvia Ostry has recently observed,

> A built-in momentum drives their rising frequency, as learning by doing generates more procedural expertise on the part of lawyers and more information by business on the opportunities the regulations afford. Designed to protect against unfair trade by restricting imports, they facilitate lobbying pressure for those with an interest in protection, including...those least favourably situated vis-à-vis their foreign competitors' costs (1990, pp. 41-42).

Negotiations would probably not be simpler if a third country were added, so a bilateral agreement offers the best chance of completion in time to a risk-averse Mexico. Though Mexico worries that the tripartite negotiating process would be more difficult and more protracted than the bilateral one, this is not a self-evident result. First, Canada has less major sources of friction with Mexico than does the U.S. The more marginal nature of the interactions between the two fringe countries guarantees that. Going through the Free Trade Agreement chapter by chapter, reveals few cases where Canada is likely to be the country arguing for the minimum amount of liberalization. In energy, for example, it is likely to be Mexico; while in transportation, it is likely to be the U.S. In most cases, Canada's less involved position is likely to leave it in its natural place: playing the part of honest broker between two others, rather than being a major protagonist itself. Second, Canada has a lot of experience in bargaining with the U.S., whose negotiators play by the rules, but play tough. Canada is a long way down the learning curve in international bargaining in general, due to being a founding member of the GATT, which Mexico only joined in 1986, and due to extensive interrelationships with the U.S. This experience may be quite helpful to Mexico at various points in the negotiations. Third, Canada's experience in specific negotiations with the U.S. administration and Congress gives it a lot of expertise and institutional organization to assist at critical times in the negotiations. For example, more than once during the Canada-U.S. Free Trade Agreement negotiations, representatives of the Canadian business community went to Washington to point out the importance of the talks and the serious consequences that would follow from a breakdown. These contacts combined with experience in using them could be as important in bringing the new negotiations to a successful conclusion as they were in the Canada-U.S. negotiations.[14]

The United States

With a bilateral agreement, the United States gains the advantages of specialization according to comparative advantage in respect to the large part of its total international trade that is done with Mexico. It also benefits from trade diversion vis-à-vis Canadian competition in the Mexican market. These same gains are achieved under a trilateral arrangement which, from the U.S. point of view, is the same as two bilateral arrangements as far as market access is concerned *except* for the absence of trade diverting effects vis-à-vis Canadian exports in the U.S. market.

A bilateral agreement makes the U.S. the preferred location for investment that serves the whole North American market because it is the only location with tariff-free access to all three markets. Under a trilateral arrangement, the U.S. becomes an attractive location for investment to serve the markets of the three countries. It does not, however, gain the preferred status that it gets with two separate bilateral agreements. Investment decisions are thus placed on a level playing field because the agreement does not bias the choice of locations among the three countries.

A bilateral agreement also promotes the U.S. politico-economic objective of helping Mexico move to a higher living standard which will, it is hoped, lead to greater political stability and democratization in that country. But these objectives will be more fully achieved by a trilateral agreement. In so far as large free market areas are better than small ones, Mexican growth gets a larger fillip from the inclusion of Canada than it gets without Canada. Furthermore, by not freezing Canada out of the second North American free trade agreement, the U.S. avoids a backlash in Canada. Initiating a movement towards a larger group of co-operating, equal partners is more likely to lead to favourable political reactions in the long run than making the U.S. the senior partner in a number of bilateral agreements negotiated on what others may come to see as a divide-and-conquer principle.

14 For details of these interventions and discussions of many other important bargaining issues, see Doern and Tomlin, 1990.

Canada

A bilateral agreement between Mexico and the U.S. means that Canada loses her preferred access to the U.S. market. As a result, any trade-diverting effects it would have obtained vis-à-vis Mexico in the U.S. market are removed. With a trilateral agreement, Canada suffers the same loss. The bilateral Free Trade Agreement gave Canada a preferred position in the U.S. market vis-à-vis any other country. The conclusion of a similar free trade agreement between the U.S. and any other country, whether or not it includes Canada, removes Canada's advantage vis-à-vis that country.

A bilateral agreement puts Canada at a competitive disadvantage vis-à-vis the U.S. as a location for investment because Canada cannot offer the tariff-free access to the Mexican market that is offered by the U.S. (which also offers tariff-free access to the Canadian market). A trilateral agreement puts Canada, the U.S., and Mexico on a more equal footing in attracting investment of establishments wishing to serve the whole North American market.

A Long-term View

Canada and Mexico have much to be gained from a trilateral agreement once the possibility of evolving to larger free trade arrangements is allowed for.

Canada and Mexico

Under the hub-and-spoke model, only the U.S. has tariff-free access to the whole area. The more spokes are added to the wheel, the more the preferred position of the U.S. is strengthened. The spoke countries, which may have common cause by virtue of being the small trading partners of one economic giant, have no chance to combine to put collective pressure on the U.S. where that is appropriate. In the case of the trade remedy laws, all countries have a common interest in resisting the U.S. Congress's tenacious defence of its tools of unilateral trade-remedy action which are often misused to become instruments of unilateral protectionism. Their use will become increasingly common in the future, and the best hope for any containment is for other countries to try to limit the worst of these within the confines of a single agreement rather than trying to do so piecemeal.

The U.S.

Economic imperialists within the U.S. Congress (and there are such persons in every country) will perceive advantages of a hub-and-spoke model as the route to U.S. hegemony over the hemisphere. For just that reason, however, the hub-and-spoke model will, in the long run, fail to meet the U.S. administration's politico-economic goals. If the U.S. wants to create the conditions that will best maintain hemispheric peace and stability, an organization of equals is required.

The only model that meets this U.S. requirement is that of plurilateral regionalism, which naturally evolves out of a trilateral free trade agreement.

How to Get the Trilateral Approach?

There are three basic ways to get to trilateral free trade, but two that create a genuine trilateral agreement which would be a route to plurilateral regionalism. The first is to negotiate two bilateral agreements, one between Mexico and the U.S, and one between Mexico and Canada. The second is to negotiate a bilateral agreement between Mexico and the U.S., and then try to trilateralize it. The third is to negotiate a trilateral agreement in the first place.

Two Bilateral Agreements

This arrangement might be possible with respect to trilateral free trade. Three separate bilateral deals, each instituting free trade but each reflecting the special bilateral concerns of the pair of countries who were signatories, would be technically feasible. At least three serious objections may, however, be raised to such an arrangement. First, it greatly enhances U.S. bargaining power, since the U.S. meets each of its spoke partners separately while they have no chance to make common cause where their interests diverge from U.S. interests. Second, since trade between Mexico and Canada is currently so small, it is doubtful that the political will would exist on both sides to persevere with the long and difficult process of reaching a bilateral agreement between Canada and Mexico. Finally, this procedure could not easily be extended to cover evolving hemispheric free trade. Agreement among even five countries would become unmanageably complex, with ten separate bilateral deals being required.

Bilateral First, then Trilateralize

This possibility has the disadvantage that the second stage of bringing Canada in could founder, either at the negotiating or the ratification stage, leaving the hub-and-spoke model in place by default.

- First, the political will may not be present in the three countries to expand the agreement to include what is currently a marginal country in terms of trade and investment flows to Mexico. The bilateral agreement gives the U.S. a privileged position in terms of being the hub of the two existing spokes with power to negotiate further spokes. Without strong political will in the U.S., neither bilateral agreement would have gone forward in spite of the obvious U.S. self-interest in each. With no obvious U.S. self-interest in converting a growing hub-and-spoke model into multilateral regionalism, the evolution must be taken as uncertain at best and a very long shot at worst (and the worst is what seems most likely). Also, Mexico will be undergoing major adjustments to the bilateral agreement with the U.S. and may not be willing to make the effort to begin negotiations with a relatively minor trading partner.

- Second, the two separate bilateral agreements will each contain their own delicately crafted compromises. None of the three countries, but in particular Canada and Mexico, will be enthusiastic about opening their agreements to serious amendment. To do so would expose themselves to further U.S. pressures to give in on some areas where they successfully resisted pressure in the now completed negotiations. It is much harder to turn two comprehensive free trade agreements into one, than to create a multilateral agreement with only one bilateral free trade agreement in existence.

Trilateral Negotiations

The preferred possibility is to make the negotiations trilateral from the outset. It is unlikely, however, that this could be done by amending the existing Canada-U.S. agreement so that Mexico could be a signatory to it. There are too many delicately crafted compromises of give and take for anyone on the Canadian or U.S. side to wish to reopen that agreement.

What is required is a new agreement that will simultaneously do several things: (i) preserve the existing Canada-U.S. Free Trade Agreement intact; (ii) provide for a trilateral free trade agreement that will give the three countries the access to each other's markets that they desire; (iii) settle specific issues (if any) between the U.S. and Mexico; and (iv) provide at least the core of an agreement to which other counties could accede.

There are many detailed ways in which this could be accomplished. I have discussed one way in an earlier publication.[15] This is to draw a core agreement from the existing Canada-U.S. agreement. The core would cover free trade in goods, and probably also the liberalization of services and investment. Mexico, and any other country, could join the free trade area by acceding to that core agreement. Each new signatory would also bargain a separate penumbra of special deals with each or all of the existing contracting parties relating to issues of special concern. I am inclined to argue for a single penumbra agreement between the new acceding party on the one hand and all the existing parties on the other. In principle, however, there could be separate penumbra agreements between the new acceding party and each of the existing parties.

15 This section relies heavily on Lipsey, 1990, pp. 9-13.

The Core Agreement

My preliminary choices for creating the core of a trilateral agreement come from chapters 1 through 6, 11, 14, 15, 17 through 19, and parts of 20 of the existing Canada-U.S. agreement. Even this selection poses some difficult problems of both inclusion and exclusion.

Chapters 1 through 6 cover the introduction on objectives, the definitions, the rules of origin, border measures, national treatment, and technical standards. These are the guts of the agreement for free trade in goods. Rules of origin may prove difficult, but will have to be settled whatever institutional route is taken. Similar comments apply to the other parts of these six core chapters.

Chapter 11 on emergency action is an important limitation to trade-restricting measures. Although Mexico may want some additional scope in this respect, the measures should be clearly sunsetted and placed in the penumbra agreement with the fundamentals of chapter 11 being the situation to be reached after any special transition measures have run their course.

Chapter 14 provides the limited, but none the less important, extension of the agreement to cover services. In the long run, as the distinction between goods and services production becomes more blurred, "free trade in goods" should routinely come to mean "free trade in goods and services." There may be some resistance from Mexico to including this chapter in the core. Again, I would favour including it, with the addition of sunsetted provisions added to the penumbra chapters to cover a transition period for Mexico—one which could be quite long.

Chapter 15, the imaginative provisions for temporary entry for business persons, should be extended without change to Mexico. However, those who worry about illegal Mexican immigration to the U.S. might make a red herring of this chapter, arguing that it was a further chink in the border.

Though I have included chapter 17 on financial services, there may be some particular special issues in this chapter that will not easily and willingly be extended to or accepted by others. Both Mexico and the U.S. have much greater restriction over their financial sectors than does Canada. All that Canada and the U.S. can probably do is to obtain national treatment for any domestic deregulation that does occur in the financial services sector.

Common dispute settlement procedures are clearly needed with respect to disagreements arising from the agreement and from changes in national laws that may impinge on the agreement. These are currently found in chapter 18. The chapter includes some special concessions made by the U.S. on such things as review of proposed legislation which it may be reluctant to extend to other countries. It would be a shame to lose the bilateral application of some of these imaginative provisions. It seems that here the U.S. must be prepared to allow precedent to rule the day by extending the chapter 18 agreements in total to other members of the free trade agreement. If it does not, it is hard to see how to proceed. Surely different provisions applying to different free trade area partners, even where the differences are small, would seem highly undesirable. Chapter 19 on the binational dispute settlement of anti-dumping and counter-vailing measures will pose problems. This is supposed to be a temporary measure while the bilateral negotiations on a subsidy code take place. If these negotiations do not reach complete agreement, the chapter 19 dispute settle-ment mechanism may well become permanent. Although it is not working perfectly, the fact that both the U.S. and Canada have chosen this route rather than the GATT mechanism shows that both sides think it a substantial improve-ment on the alternative multilateral dispute settlement mechanism (which I have no doubt that it is). Will the trilateral negotiations set the bilateral ones to one side? Will the U.S. be willing to make the chapter 19 dispute settlement mechanism trilateral, thus risking that Mexican and Canadian arbitrators will make common cause against what they perceive as the misuse of U.S. fair trade laws to act as non-tariff barriers? Whatever the answers to these and other similar pressing questions, some common method of settling such disputes surely needs to be a part of any trilateral free trade agreement. Two significantly different mechanisms for settling disputes over the application of fair trade laws would cause invidious comparisons and continued friction with the partner who thought it was covered by the inferior mechanism. None the less, it will not be easy to extend the chapter 19 mechanism to Mexico since that country does not have the procedure of determination by quasi judicial bodies combined with appeals to higher courts that is found in both the U.S. and Canada.

The Penumbra

Exclusions from the core also pose problems. I excluded chapters 7 on agricul-ture, 9 on energy, 13 on government procurement, 16 on investment, and 20 (2005) on cultural industries. All of these have some carefully crafted compro-mises relating to points of bilateral friction. Mexico's special interests will hardly lead it to want to accede to these provisions without revision. In some cases, it may want more restrictions (e.g., possibly in energy and autos) and in other cases, it will want fewer restrictions (e.g., probably in cultural industries).

Perhaps something should be said about the contentious chapter 9 on energy which, according to the critics, no supplying country would want to accept. This clause has been widely misinterpreted, both in Canada and in Mexico, as meaning that in some way or another, control over Canadian energy has been signed over to the U.S. The chapter certainly was one of the most controversial in the agreement. It pitted the energy exporting provinces, who supported it, against many lobbyists in the energy importing provinces, who opposed it because it would prevent them from legislating consumption of Canadian energy at below world prices to their benefit, and at the producing provinces cost.

The chapter covers a large number of energy products, including coal, coal gas, crude oil, petroleum products, natural gas, uranium, electricity (which is not covered by the GATT), and liquified petroleum gases such as propane, butane and ethane. It does not cover water—in spite of many allegations still being made by the critics.

Basically, the chapter institutionalizes the current regime of free trade in energy products. This is something that free traders support but interventionists oppose. Beyond that, it commits each country to the minimum behaviour on both the demand and the supply side that would allow each to be willing to rely on the other as major demanders or suppliers. The United States agrees to restrict the use of national defence as a reason for cutting off demand through government decree—it has been done in the past. It does this by defining national security, in Article 907, much more narrowly than under the GATT. It also agrees (along with Canada) to give the other partner the right to formal consultation over any changes in regulatory policies that distort energy trade. It also reduces the possibility of countervailing duties being levied against fiscal incentive for exploration.

Article 904 aroused much controversy in Canada: it allows export restrictions, consistent with GATT obligations, and subject to the following provisions:

- The restriction does not prevent the other country from having access to the same proportion of the total domestic supply of that good which it received in the most recent 36-month period prior.
- It does not use measures, such as licence fees, taxation, or minimum price requirements, to impose prices for exports that exceed prices charged in the domestic market (except where higher prices result from action under the previous point).
- The restriction does not require the disruption of normal channels of supply.

Basically, what this section does is to embed the articles of the GATT with a few exceptions into a more obligatory document making it explicit that these obligations cover energy products.

The proportional access rule was, however, heavily criticised as a sell out of control over Canadian energy. Nothing so drastic seems to be implied by this proportional sharing rule. Consider the following. First, the rule has no effect under normal conditions. Second, it comes into play only if the exporting country wishes to declare an emergency sufficiently urgent to justify interfering with normal commercial contracts. If so, the exporting country must cut back on sales in proportion to existing contracts. This arrangement would seem to be the minimum guarantee that is needed on the supply side if the U.S. is willing to rely on Canada to supply important parts of its energy supplies. For example, if a nuclear accident curtailed electricity output in Ontario, the provincial government could not dictate that all supplies be cut off from New York state in order to keep up full supplies to Canadian customers. Instead, if production was cut back, say by 30 percent, both foreign and domestic customers would have to share proportionally in that 30 percent reduction. Without this insurance against any arbitrary shutting off the tap by governments in the suppliers jurisdiction, the users might be unwilling to rely on foreign supplies for their energy. Since Canadians wish to sell energy to the U.S., they are willing, as suppliers, to make this commitment.

Here are a few of the commonly made assertions about the sharing agreement that are manifestly wrong, but which the critics continue to assert none the less: (i) the energy sharing agreement gives the U.S. preferred access to Canada's resource supplies; (ii) the proportional sharing agreement stops Canada from having an independent policy on such matters as the conservation of scarce supplies of natural resources and the appropriation of resource rents when these are high; (iii) the agreement means that if Canada sells some quantity of energy (say electricity) to the U.S., Canada must go on selling that amount for all future times. All of these assertions and many more like them are wrong.[16]

So much for what might be in the penumbra. It would also be necessary to decide how the non-core chapters were to be negotiated, and whether or not they were to be embodied in a single trilateral agreement or separate bilateral ones. These problems could get unmanageably complex as the number of countries and the number of issues that were accepted to be special, increase.

Another important principle should be to sunset virtually all exceptions and special provisions that depart from the principle of free trade in goods and services. The motto here should be "never say 'never' just say 'a very long time'." The Canadian and American negotiators would have been well advised to apply this in the bilateral case: exclude something for 50 years if you must, but never exclude it forever. Time discounts are such that even strong special interest groups will often settle for protection in their own lifetimes. Time, however, ticks on inexorably, and an agreement with no "nevers" but only some "very long exclusion times" would slowly evolve to a complete, unequivocal free trade area. (Think, for example, of the great boon to the world if instead of giving in to French pressure and adopting the common agricultural policy (the

16 For a detailed analysis of these and other allegations, see Lipsey and York, 1988.

CAP) indefinitely, Germany had insisted on sunsetting the measures after 40 years. That would have seemed forever in 1958, but as 1998 comes nearer, the difference between never including agriculture in free trade and including it after 40 years would seem more and more important.)

The Dividing Line

The above discussion suggests one principle that might help delineate the core from the penumbra and also help strengthen the core. The core would be based on the principles of full free trade in goods and services. This would be the end to which the actual free trade area would evolve when all sunsetted provisions had expired. The penumbra would contain a set of exceptions, phase-in allowances, adjustment provisions, and special cases. In all possible cases these would be sunsetted (over 50 or 75 years if necessary) rather than being permanent. The number of permanent special provisions would be kept to a bare minimum. Over time, the penumbra would wither away leaving trade among the partners to be governed mainly by the core.

This procedure would mean that there would be only one core agreement, one which would be signed by each new entrant at the time of entry. There would also be only one penumbra agreement for each country. This agreement would be negotiated between each new entrant and all of the existing members of the free trade area. At any one time, however, there would be a series of old penumbra agreements, each applying to one member, negotiated at the time of that member's entry, and each slowly eroding as its particular sunsetting provisions come into play.

Evolution to a Customs Union, A Common Market, and Beyond

Finally, many see a free trade area as only the first step to closer economic and even political unions. What are the prospects for a free trade agreement between Mexico, the U.S., and Canada evolving into one or another of these closer economic relationships?

We have already argued that it is quite likely that a tripartite agreement would evolve into a more geographically extended free trade area that, in the limit, could cover all of the Western Hemisphere. It is a major argument of this paper that this possibility needs to be foreseen now and institutions that would facilitate it should be put into place now.

But what of the other kind of extension, not of the geographical extent of the existing type of agreement, but to a fuller type of co-operation between existing contracting bodies. The first logical progression from a free trade area is to a common market. This first step, however, would seem to be the most difficult step for a free trade area of Western Hemisphere countries that includes the U.S. A customs union has to have harmonized external barriers to the movement of goods (and, in modern times, services as well). The problem is that as a world superpower, the U.S. has often used trade and investment restrictions as political tools in ways that other potential members of the free trade area have disapproved. For example, neither Canada nor Mexico supported the U.S. embargoes on trade with communist China in the 1950s and with Cuba that continues into the 1990s. In general, for a large country such as the U.S., trade policy is often an instrument of foreign policy. In contrast, for a small country such as Canada, for which trade is a life and death matter, foreign policy is often an instrument of trade policy.[17]

By virtue of its unequal economic power, and its important place as a great superpower, the United States would have the major say in the external trade barriers of any customs union covering any number of the countries in the Western Hemisphere. Since Canada, and no doubt many other potential members of such a union, would be unwilling to subject themselves to U.S. decisions on such matters as trade with Cuba, a customs union seems unlikely to gain political approval.

This raises an interesting question, not often asked before: can one have a common market, or any closer form of economic integration, without the common external barriers to trade implied by a customs union? My answer is: "why not?" There would be a cumbersome aspect to a "non-customs union common market," but if the member countries are willing to pay that price in order to preserve their commercial policy independence vis-à-vis third countries, then what is to stand in their way?

A common market is almost in place now on investment. The globalization of world competition, and the growth of TNCs with home-bases in many countries, is fast resulting in free flows of capital through much of the world. Furthermore, the sophistication of globalized financial markets, combined with the ability of TNCs to move funds across borders but within one firm, makes most of the capital flow restrictions that were used to buttress the fixed exchange rate regimes of the 1950s and 1960s unworkable today. Most countries still have some restrictions on foreign ownership, particularly in such key industries as communications, energy, and transportation. They also often reserve the ability to review foreign take-overs of domestic firms. (Currently the U.S. has no such restrictions, while Canada's review of U.S. take-overs is limited to firms larger than $150 million by the terms of the Free Trade Agreement.)

---

17 This point is elaborated in Grey, 1981.

Virtually all economists and most governments—to judge by their behaviour—accept the value of both inward and outward bound foreign investment. As we observed earlier, however, there is current debate as to the desirability of allowing completely free capital movements. Many modern theories of growth, under conditions of increasing returns to scale, non-existence of static equilibrium, hysteresis effects, and positive feedback systems, leave a potential for small interventions into investment decision to have very large effects over a decade or so. Observers who place importance on these newer theories argue that it is misguided for any country to abandon all control over investment flows. Others feel that a liberal regime with complete free flows of investment is the goal towards which policy should strive—even if it never quite gets there.

Whatever the outcome of this debate, a free de facto flow of investment consistent with a common market is not too far off what now happens between Canada and the U.S—with certain ownership restrictions in sensitive industries. Presumably, this will also be not far off what will be happening in Mexico once the current bout of reforms is completed.

The more the number of countries included, and the more unequal their current levels of economic development, the more will be the resistance to going to a regime of completely free capital flows.

If capital flows will pose a minor problem in moving to a common market, labour flows are likely to pose a major one, at least at the political level. Hecksher-Ohlin theory states that trade and factor flows are substitutes for each other: free flows of either goods or factors will equalize factor incomes internationally. This theory is based, however, on the crucial assumption that production functions are identical in all countries. Most modern attempts to explain what we see in international patterns of relative productivity levels and their rates of growth make use of differences in production functions. The reason is that technological advance is centred in a few countries, and then diffuses slowly throughout the world. This diffusion process is costly and time consuming. To "copy" an innovation from another country requires substantial adaptation of the original process and that requires some amount of local R&D capacity. This appears to be true both for copying from one country to another, and even from one firm to another within one country.[18] Under such circumstances, free trade in goods will not succeed in equalizing factor incomes and

18 I list only three of the many references that cover this and related points which bear critically on the issues of the causes of differential growth rates among existing countries and to the effects of removing barriers to factor movements among countries. See Porter, 1990; Mowrey and Rosenberg, 1989; and Dosi, Pavitt, and Soete, 1990.

there will be an economic incentive for emigration from lower to higher productivity countries. If factor movements are determined solely by factor incomes, the movement will continue until factor incomes are equalized. If the high-productivity country is large relative to the low-productivity country, this may be a politically acceptable result. If the reverse is true, the small high-productivity country may be unwilling to see its factor income lowered by migration almost to those of the large low-productivity country. For example, the countries of the EC are currently wondering how to raise barriers to the immigration of millions of people once the U.S.S.R. eliminates its prohibitive barriers to emigration.

This argument ignores two types of considerations. First, there are dynamic effects. Although in a static world, free migration lowers the real wages of some factors of production, an arrangement that increases the rate of economic growth may make all income earners better off within a decade. Surely, for example, virtually all of the residents of countries such as Argentina would be better off today if, 40 years ago, the adminstration had adopted growth maximizing policies rather than worrying about the fairness of the distribution of the existing level of national income.

Second, there are many important non-economic considerations. When these are introduced, migration does not necessarily eliminate differentials in labour earnings. If citizens of the low-income country prefer living in that society because, for example, of language and cultural considerations, they may emigrate temporarily to the higher income country, remaining only long enough to save some targeted capital sum. This has been the case, for example, with the free movement of labour between high-income U.K. and the lower-income Republic of Ireland. Irish workers typically come to the U.K., remain for around ten years, and then return home. As a result, the net flow of Irish immigrants is vastly smaller than the gross flow. Something similar may happen between Mexico and the U.S. with many Mexicans returning to the home country after spending a period of time in the U.S.

A common market that included the free flow of labour among its provisions would affect that flow for several reasons. First, the flow would be reduced from the supply side because Mexican real incomes would rise rapidly, thus reducing the incentive to emigrate. Second, the flow would be reduced from the demand side because Mexican workers in the U.S. would all be legal workers who would have to be paid the minimum wage and all the fringe costs and benefits that raise the cost to employers well above the wage actually paid. On the other hand, the flow would be increased from the supply side because people who are currently deterred by the need to cross the border by clandestine methods would be more willing to cross. What would happen to the net flow is not known but more research is needed on what now happens between Mexico and the U.S. and across other borders subject to fewer restrictions. It is not inconceivable, however, that contrary to alarmist fears, the free movement of labour combined with an acceleration in Mexican economic growth would result in a smaller net flow of immigrants from Mexico to the U.S. than now occurs.

The more countries that are included, and the wider the current discrepancies in their productivity levels, the more the high-income partners would fear massive immigration from lower income partners. Whatever the ethics and the economics of the situation, the politics would probably dictate that a free trade area would come first, and only after income levels had narrowed significantly would free movement of labour be contemplated.

This timing could set up a conflict between extending the free trade area to cover more countries, many of which would be at lower productivity levels, and turning the free trade area between the existing countries into a more embracing arrangement. For example, it is quite conceivable that Mexico could be on a sufficiently rapid growth path ten years from now that a common market could be politically contemplated. If, at that time, an extension to other lower-productivity countries in Central or South America were contemplated, the common market might be postponed.

If a common market were possible, there would seem to be no overriding reason why a currency union might not follow. Integration along the lines of Europe 1992 and further, would require a willingness to curtail national sovereignty substantially in ways that would be quite unacceptable to electorates in Canada, the U.S., or Mexico today. No one can guess, however, how opinion will evolve over 100 years.

The Outlook for the Hemisphere

Although we must hope that the multilateral system will continue to prosper, that should not preclude our trying other avenues which may realize major regional plurilateral liberalizations. The European Community has pointed the way for such regional trade liberalization. Latin America has, to some extent, been bypassed by the globalizing winds that are blowing through the world economy. The old inward-looking policies are discredited. Certainly, the experiences of other areas show that the surest route to high living standards is to have large tariff-free domestic markets, and to take part in the world division of labour as produced by the present activities of TNCs.

Latin America has tried many inward-looking policies directed at economic growth. Possibly now is the time to give outward-looking policies a chance. The hemisphere's resource potential is enormous—at least on a scale with Europe's. If human resources can be mobilized, and the advantages of specialization in a vast barrier-free market of over 400 million people realized, surely the sky is the limit. Or, to be more conservative, there seems no reason why the residents of Latin America should not aspire to have within their lifetime living standards as high, and poverty levels as low as those now found in the EC. It is a worthy aspiration to realize the vast economic potential of the hemisphere.

References

Doern, G.B. and Brian W. Tomlin, "Faith and Fear: The Free Trade Story," mimeo, Ottawa: Carleton University, 1990.

Dosi, Giovanni, Keith Pavitt, and Luc Soete, *The Economics of Technical Change and International Trade*, Hemel Hempstead, England: Harvester Wheatsheaf, 1990.

Grey, Rodney, *Trade Policy in the 1980s: An Agenda for Canada-U.S. Trade Relations*, Montreal: C.D. Howe Institute, 1981.

Lipsey, R.G., *Canada at the Mexico-U.S. Free Trade Negotiations: Wallflower or Partner*, Toronto: C.D. Howe Institute, 1990.

Lipsey, R.G. and W. Dobson, eds., *Shaping Comparative Advantage*, Toronto: C.D. Howe Institute, 1986.

Lipsey, R.G. and M. Smith, "The Canadian-U.S. Free Trade Agreement: Special Case or Wave of The Future?" in J.J. Schott, ed., *Free Trade Areas and U.S. Trade Policy*, Washington, D.C.: Institute for International Affairs, 1989.

Lipsey, R.G. and R. York, *Evaluating the Free Trade Deal: A Guided Tour Through the Canada-U.S. Agreement*, Toronto: C.D. Howe Institute, 1988.

Mowrey, David and Nathan Rosenberg, *Technology and the Pursuit of Economic Growth*, Cambridge: Cambridge University Press, 1989.

Ostry, Sylvia, *Governments and Corporations in a Shrinking World: Trade and Innovation Policies in the United States, Europe and Japan*, New York: Council on Foreign Relations Press, 1990.

Porter, Michael E., *The Competitive Advantage of Nations*, New York: The Free Press, 1990.

Smith, Murray G., ed., *Global Rivalry and Intellectual Property: Developing Canadian Strategies*, Ottawa: The Institute for Research on Public Policy, 1991.

United Nations, *Transnational Corporations in World Development: Trends and Prospects*, New York, 1988.

Chapter 5

Lessons from the European Experience

Rosemary P. Piper and Alan Reynolds

Just as the architects of the European integration experiment looked to the United States and its strong federalist traditions for direction, now North America can turn to Europe for insight into the process of economic integration. This paper evaluates the past experience and future expectations of the European single market, with the hope of facilitating a smoother, more rapid integration of the economies of North America. By emulating the successes of Europe, and avoiding similar setbacks, the recent, relatively modest moves toward free trade agreements between Canada, the United States, and Mexico can become the start of a far more significant and productive North American common market (NACM).

The most important lesson North America can learn from Europe is that economic integration is quite feasible, without nations forfeiting their cultural identity, without widespread migration of people toward more affluent countries, and without mass relocation of manufacturing activities to low-wage countries. During more than 40 years of development, the European Community (EC) enterprise has proved most successful when it first secures a binding pre-commitment from members, builds on concrete achievements, and takes care not to interfere unnecessarily on issues of national sovereignty. The results can be tremendous. Membership in the EC has brought much larger economic and political gains than expected.

The Early Evolution Toward a Common Market

The ongoing evolution toward a European Common Market began shortly after the Second World War as a seemingly unpromising gesture toward co-operative relations among recent enemies. Despite this implausible beginning, and the scepticism it continuously inspired, there has been enormous and accelerating progress toward breaking down barriers between an increasing number of European nations. A dozen nations of the European Community already constitute an economic powerhouse with a combined output larger than that of the United States, a population larger than the Soviet Union, and exports outside the EC ($430 billion in 1989) larger than those of the entire Asia-Pacific region ($400 billion).

The process of opening markets and eliminating impediments to trade among sovereign states raises several critical challenges. The newly formed economic entity must balance diversity of national interests against the benefits of joining a larger regional bloc (for example the contrast between floating exchange rates and currency co-ordination). It must consider the best level of government from which to make effective policy (for example, professional qualifications for physicians). It must weigh the relative importance of national sovereignty versus organizational unity (as with the elimination of security checks at internal borders).

Such concerns prevented the European countries from stepping forward in one large leap to full integration. Would it really prove economically viable to each specific country? Would bigger countries dominate? By building slowly to a common market through a process of modest lasting steps, the countries involved gradually learned the economic benefits of integration. As Robert Schuman, the French foreign minister, said in 1950, "Europe would not be made all at once or according to a single general plan. It will be built through concrete achievements, which first create a *de facto* solidarity."

In 1951 the foundation for the European Community was laid with the creation of a European Coal and Steel Community (ECSC) to control the basic materials needed to make war, and to bind Germany firmly into the European political and economic alliance. The ECSC developed true supranational institutions, improved relations between member states, and consequently convinced Europeans—both politicians and their constituencies—that economic integration was possible and even worthwhile.

Ironically, one of the major political setbacks in the history of the European Community, the European Defense Community (EDC), is partially responsible for the progress made by the European Community in recent years. With the outbreak of the Korean War in 1950 and heightening tensions between East and West, plans for an integrated military were pushed quickly through the negotiating process and the EDC treaty was signed in May 1952.

When tensions declined after Stalin died in 1953, the enormity of what the EDC proposed dawned on the French National Assembly, and the country that had originated the plan refused to ratify it. The EDC would have called for common supranational institutions, a common budget, and common armed forces.

In retrospect, the overly ambitious EDC plan illustrated the need to avoid initiatives which too directly compromise national sovereignty, particularly with respect to foreign policy. The EDC also demonstrated that strategies concentrating on economic integration would be much less contentious than those attempting to forge political integration. Just a few years later, the European Economic Community was successfully formed with the Treaty of Rome.

Ratified in 1957, the Treaty of Rome committed the six signatories (West Germany, France, Italy, The Netherlands, Belgium, and Luxembourg) to the creation of a common internal market. Its wording combined the narrow, practical strategies necessary for achieving a "customs union" (the elimination of internal tariffs and the development of a common external tariff within 12 years), with more expansive rhetoric calling for a true "common market" (free movement of labour and capital) or "economic union" (including a common monetary policy). The treaty also created the framework for common agricultural, transport, and regional development policies.

Following the Treaty of Rome, the most important success was the elimination of tariffs and import quotas between members of the community, accomplished by 1968 (e.g., tariffs were cut 10 percent per year). Other positive steps included the 1970 introduction of the community budget system to raise revenues (primarily for agricultural and development funds), the 1979 formation of the European Monetary System to strengthen currency stability, and the beginning of direct elections for the European Parliament, also in 1979. Meanwhile, the size of the community grew. Ireland, Denmark, and the United Kingdom joined in 1973, Greece joined in 1981, and Spain and Portugal in 1986, bringing the community to its current total of 12 nations.

Figure 1 shows the concrete results from the liberalization of EC trade. Trade volume soared, becoming an ever-increasing percentage of member countries' output and income. Trade outside the EC also increased relative to GDP, until recent years. Tougher competition from Asia and North America revealed setbacks in the liberalization and integration of European commerce. There was much left to do.

While member states had dismantled tariffs as stipulated under the Treaty of Rome, they simultaneously had undermined its spirit by developing divergent technical standards, imposing national restrictions on government procurement, and subsidizing such industries as steel, textiles, automobiles, and a

Figure 1
European Community Export of Goods
As a Percent of GDP

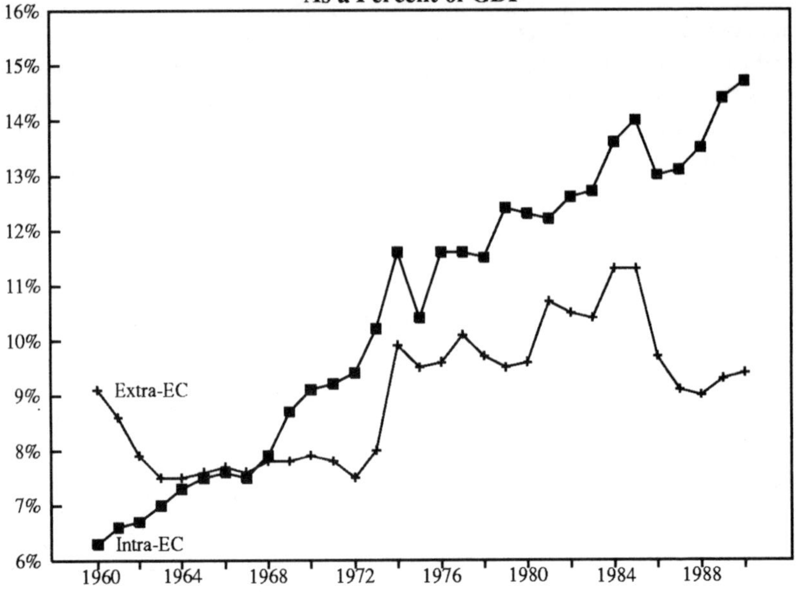

Source: European Commission, November 1989.

host of others.[1] Such subsidies were permitted under EC treaties on the pretext that the decline of these industries would cause "politically unacceptable levels of unemployment."

As a result, Philips N.V. produces seven types of television sets to meet differing national standards on voltage, semiconductors, and tuners.[2] Airlines based in one member country are still restricted from offering domestic flights in another member country.[3] Public purchasing, accounting for nearly 15 percent of EC GNP, is still awarded to national firms in 98 percent of all cases.[4]

Not only did member countries find ways to protect home markets in manners accepted under the Treaty of Rome, they also increasingly violated explicit treaty provisions. The number of cases of noncompliance, where a

1   See, for example, European Commission, *Second Survey on State Aids in the European Community*, 1990.

2   See Hufbauer, 1990, p. 6.

3   Betts, 1990, p. 4.

4   U.S. Department of Commerce, 1990, p. xi.

country was accused of protecting a specific market from imports, shot up from 50 in 1970 to 289 in 1983.[5]

Based on this early history of the EC, several implications can be drawn for a North American Common Market. First, progress comes by setting visionary, but realistic goals and building gradually on successes. Second, confounding economic and political integration, especially at the early stages, can derail the process. Third, removing trade barriers alone will not be sufficient to bring about the remarkable benefits of a single market. While a North American free trade agreement is an important first step to integration, the most worthwhile gains will come from a concerted effort to remove trade impediments that lie behind borders.

Toward 1992

Europe's program of integration had languished in the 1970s when two oil crises, inflation, and recession rocked its economy. Between 1974 and 1984, growth of gross domestic product (GDP) in Europe averaged an anaemic 1.5 percent per year and average European unemployment grew to over 10 percent. On top of this, inflation differentials between countries increased, ranging from 4 percent in West Germany to 17 percent in Italy, which made currency co-ordination difficult, yet also more essential. Moreover, new members widened the size of the community, but compromised its ability to introduce deeper reforms.

Protectionism, floating exchange rates, and economic planning of the 1970s had failed to deliver the promised economic progress. At the same time, rapid technological change and increased competition from the U.S., Japan, and the Asian NIC's challenged continental Europe to find a cure for its economic malaise. The Reagan and Thatcher governments' emphasis on deregulation, privatization, and tax reform helped revive Europe's interest in freer markets. By the mid-1980s, it became apparent that Europe's failure to complete its plans for an integrated market was costing it billions in lost opportunities.

Jacques Delors, formerly a French finance minister and president of the EC Commission since 1985, played a critical role in restarting the EC integration process. He commissioned the June 1985 White Paper, *Completing the Internal Market*, which laid the groundwork for the EC 1992 program, outlining 300 measures needed to complete EC integration.

The Single European Act, ratified in February 1986, facilitated the implementation of the 300 provisions of the White Paper. It set the deadline of December 31, 1992, for removal of the remaining obstacles to the European

5   Drouin, Ernst, and Wheeler, 1987, p. 76.

Common Market. It simplified the cumbersome decision-making apparatus of the community by allowing for greater use of majority voting in place of unanimity. It added issues to the community's agenda, including the co-ordination of policies concerning currencies, research and development, the environment, and social issues.

Three strategies formed the basis of the EC 1992 project and have proved critical to its success:

- First, the leaders of the EC 1992 project established a credible program. Member countries made a commitment to its goals, through the passage of the Single European Act. EC policy-makers established an ambitious timetable and made sincere efforts to stick to it. All of the 279 proposals conceived in the 1985 White Paper have been drafted and submitted by the European Commission, the executive body of the EC, and over 60 percent of them have been adopted by the Council, its final decision-making body.[6] This strategy was borrowed from Jean Monnet, one of the original architects of the EC, who believed that European unification would only progress if clear objectives and a rigid schedule were established.

- Second, they left the negotiation of priorities to the ongoing bargaining process. The establishment of priorities inevitably favours the interests of one member country over another. By refusing at the outset to establish a set order for consideration of the 300 proposals, the EC left an important bargaining point to the negotiating parties. This strategy helped thwart the well-known delaying tactic of questioning priorities. It also recognized that the push toward integration would be unbalanced, progressing easily in some directions and with difficulty in others. The absence of priorities, and the wide scope of issues on the table, allowed the unfolding of the integration program to occur in ways that were perhaps unpredictable, but more palatable.

- Third, they maintained some ambiguity in purpose. Each country has its own distinct reasons for belonging to the community, and these motivations evolve over time. The United Kingdom sees the EC process as a way to cement the deregulation efforts of the Thatcher era throughout Europe. France sees EC 1992 as a way to constrain the economic dominance of Germany. Germany sees an integrated Europe as an enormous business opportunity to supply capital equipment needed to invigorate less affluent economies. Spain sees

6   EC Bulletin, August 31, 1990, p. 3.

the process as an express route to modernization. The union thus permits some healthy diversity in purpose, and some uncertainty in ultimate goals, to satisfy each of the members.[7]

The successful formation of a NACM will also require a credible program that sets common goals and a strict timetable, while maintaining flexibility in the speed and direction at which integration occurs and the reasons behind each member's participation. What has made the EC 1992 project work is the very fact that there is substance behind the rhetoric.

Goals of 1992

The EC 1992 program targets for removal three different categories of barriers; technical, fiscal, and physical. Technical barriers refer to divergent national product standards and cover such diverse areas as financial regulation, health and safety regulations, and nationally protected public procurement markets. Fiscal barriers result from substantial differences in value-added taxes (VAT) and excise duties among the different EC members. Physical barriers refer to the red tape and delays that impede cross-border movement. Despite the completion of the European customs union in 1968, the EC countries must maintain border controls to adjust for differences in value-added tax rates and farm prices (fluctuations in exchange rates distort fixed EC-wide prices), and to monitor bilateral trade agreements with non-EC countries in such areas as textiles and cars.

Institutional Arrangements

To carry out its internal market program, the EC usually issues directives, which compel national governments to implement corresponding legislation in their home country. The directives are drafted by the European Commission, composed of 17 commissioners appointed by their national governments, but explicitly told to maintain a pan-EC (supranational) perspective. A staff of nearly 13,000 assists them.

The Commission submits proposals for review by the Council of Ministers, an intergovernmental body which includes top-level ministers from each country. This body, meeting two times per year, has the power to veto Commission proposals. It has been termed the "brake" to integration because each member maintains a distinct national perspective. A staff of 2,000 assists them.

EC institutions tend to be elitist rather than democratic for reasons of efficiency. The European Commission, with its *appointed* members, and the

---

7   Hoffman, 1989, p. 39.

Council of Ministers, made up of national leaders, initiate all proposals. The European Parliament, with its 518 *elected* members, is mainly consultative.

The EC governing structure has improved because of its adaptability. For example, the Single European Act, which took effect July 1987, permitted more use of majority voting in the Council of Ministers. No longer could one country hold up the entire process. The Single European Act also enhanced the role of the European Parliament, giving it the power to require a unanimous vote in the Council of Ministers. Parliament's power is likely to increase further, as the EC assumes more control over political issues.

Accomplishments to Date

The EC 1992 program is ambitious in scope and timetable. It has already produced some radical breakthroughs. Border crossing has been made easier through the Single Administration Document, which cut the number of required documents from as many as 100 to one. EC citizens not only can work in any member country, but their families are free to join them and their social security benefits will follow. As of July 1, 1990, countries are no longer permitted to restrict capital movements (though a liberal safeguard provision and phase-in period for poorer countries is included). Banks and insurance companies may set up operations across borders, governed by the supervisory rules in their home country. After 1992, quotas on road haulage, which affected 50 percent of all bilateral trips, will be phased out. In the area of public procurement, which accounts for as much as 15 percent of EC GNP, governments must advertise the larger opportunities, use common standards, and report who wins a bid.

Mutual Recognition of Standards

The principle of mutual recognition, applied in nearly 70 percent of the EC directives approved to date, is an especially noteworthy aspect of the 1992 program.[8] Initially, the EC looked to full harmonization of technical regulations. The ultimately unsuccessful proposal for a "Euroloaf," with its legislated bread ingredients, demonstrated the folly of this approach. In some cases, harmonization locked in inefficient technical standards which lagged international ones and therefore created a barrier to external competition.

In the mid-1980s "mutual recognition" replaced harmonization. Mutual recognition called for countries within the community to agree on a basic set of standards for health, safety, and the environment. Beyond this, each country would accept products that comply with the regulations of other member countries. Because of mutual recognition, the French can now buy Italian

8   European Commission, June-July 1989, p. 5.

salami, and French Creme de Cassis liqueur (which had been prohibited due to low alcohol content) is now available in Germany. Mutual recognition forces regulatory systems to compete—whether in applying rules to banks, doctors, or computers. Its introduction drastically accelerated the integration process.

For North America to simply turn to EC-style mutual recognition of technical standards would be a significant achievement. The U.S.-Canada Free Trade Agreement adopted the principle of national treatment, limiting the types of goods and services sold across borders to those which meet the regulations of the host country. While this approach steers clear of any infringement on sovereignty, it does little to remove barriers to trade, and limits the competition between countries over standards.

The European Monetary System

Another great accomplishment of the European integration movement has been the formation of the European Monetary System (EMS). Established in 1979, the EMS promotes exchange rate stability through informal policy co-ordination among national central banks. Currencies of member countries are permitted to fluctuate 2.25 percent relative to other EC currencies (except for Italy and Britain which are allowed fluctuations of +/- 6 percent).

Until about 1986, France, Italy, Denmark, and Ireland repeatedly devalued against the strong German mark and Dutch guilder. All they had to show for this exercise in independence, though, was higher inflation and higher interest rates. Foreign investors naturally learned to demand higher bond yields to compensate for the risk of exchange rate losses, while domestic investors likewise sought to protect their capital by holding foreign or tangible assets as a "hedge" against inflation. After 1986, increased compliance with the discipline of keeping exchange rates in line with the German and Dutch currencies has brought impressive convergence of EC inflation rates, as shown in figure 2.

Volatility of exchange rates within the EMS has fallen sharply, while such volatility has increased outside the EMS, and between EMS and non-EMS currencies.[9] As a consequence, the EMS has been able to avoid frequent and large currency realignments. Out of five realignments since 1983, only two involved more than one currency, a remarkable achievement given the size and scope of the system. Fewer exchange rate fluctuations mean lower transaction costs and reduced uncertainty in cross-border trade and investment. As people in countries that formerly experienced high and erratic inflation become more

9   See McDonald and Zis, March 1989, p. 184; and Ungerer, Evans, Mayer, and Young, 1986.

Figure 2
Inflation Rates
(Percent Change in GDP price deflator)

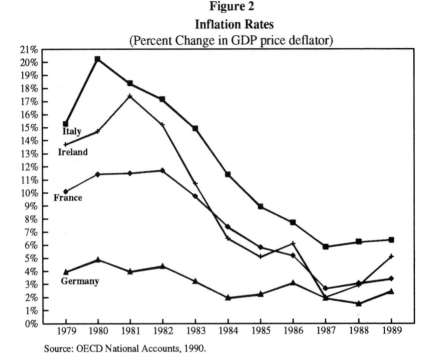

Source: OECD National Accounts, 1990.

confident in their currency, they become more willing to save at lower interest rates.

In the fall of 1990, the British government, faced with 11 percent inflation and 14 percent interest rates, finally announced that it would bring the pound within the exchange rate mechanism (ERM). Yet the other 11 EC members soon pushed further ahead, with new plans to move to a full economic and monetary union (EMU) and European central bank. The ultimate goal is to share a common currency, as exists among the 50 United States, with many of the same commercial advantages of sharing a common language (i.e., lower costs of information and transactions).

Britain balked once again, apparently because of anxiety about the need to devalue if high inflation makes British goods uncompetitive, causing a trade deficit.[10] Yet this Keynesian analysis is inappropriate to a true common market. Due to competitive pressures, a common market country with a credible

10 See, for example, Swann, 1990, pp. 181, 196.

commitment to eschew devaluation cannot sustain a faster inflation. British worries about the need to "deflate" actually refer to the need to refrain from inflating, on the discredited notion that inflation keeps unemployment down. Moreover, the typical anxiety about payments "imbalances" would be irrelevant within an economic and monetary union. Nobody in the U.S. worries if New York City's chronic deficit on merchandise trade is properly balanced with a surplus in services and capital in-flows.

According to a 1990 European Commission study, monetary union would eliminate exchange rate variability which still amounts to an average monthly rate of 0.7 percent for EMS currencies against all other EC currencies. The study also estimates that lower transaction costs would add 0.5 percent to community GNP. Other intangible benefits identified, but not quantified, include price stability, less vulnerability to sudden shifts in demand for a country's products, more pressure for budgetary discipline, and greater attention to structural adjustments, not devaluation, to promote growth.[11]

Prospects for the Post-1992 Period

While on paper, the European Commission has done a tremendous job approving the directives required for the single internal market, the true test will be in the implementation and enforcement of these provisions.

At the end of February 1990, 90 EC laws had reached their implementation date, yet action has been uneven by the legislatures in member countries. The United Kingdom and Denmark have been the most punctual, implementing 77 out of all 90 directives. Italy and Portugal, on the other hand, have implemented 36 and 37, respectively.[12]

By the target date of December 31, 1992, despite substantial progress made in removing intra-EC barriers, impediments will remain. Border crossings will become even easier and cheaper, but problems of drugs, immigration, and terrorism will necessitate continued intra-EC border controls. Several of the poorest EC countries are likely to continue to restrict capital mobility. They have promised, however, to remove all restrictions by 1995. While the EC record on public procurement legislation has been excellent, many local and regional governments are likely to ignore new rules which could hurt powerful local interests. Enforcement will be critical to further progress. Clearly, implementation of the Europe 1992 program will continue well into the next century. Particularly sticky issues, in addition to monetary union, are agricultural support, taxation, social policy, and external trade relations.

11 Commission of the European Communities, October 1990, p. 20.
12 European Commission, *Target 92*, 1990, p. 3.

Unresolved Issues

Agricultural Policy

In the early 1960s Europe introduced a common agricultural policy (CAP) to protect farmers from declining incomes and fluctuations in world farm prices. Through a system of price support and stabilization policies, the CAP has achieved some of its objectives. Prices of EC farm products have risen to nearly twice world levels and EC food production has grown, expanding at an average annual rate of 2 percent. (Meanwhile consumption has only been increasing by 0.5 percent.)[13] In fact, production incentives have been so successful that they have lead to huge surpluses of some products and the notorious beef, milk, and butter mountains.

The CAP's qualified successes have been achieved at enormous cost. The program now swallows over 60 percent of the EC budget ($33 billion), transferring funds to some of Europe's wealthiest countries. From 1968 to 1988, agriculture declined as a share of GNP (from 7 percent to 3.5 percent) and as a share of employment (from 12 percent to 2.6 percent), yet EC spending on agriculture as a percent of GNP rose 46 percent.[14]

Moreover, the CAP costs European consumers billions more in higher prices as well as higher taxes. Overpriced food makes Europeans poorer, less able to buy other goods and services. Economists estimate that the CAP's inefficiencies (or deadweight loss) waste approximately 1 percent of EC GNP annually.[15] Just as damaging, higher farm prices divert scarce financial and human resources from more competitive sectors. In response to mounting surpluses and escalating costs, the EC has made several efforts to reform the CAP. It has restricted EC agricultural spending, set production ceilings, and introduced a set-aside program to pay farmers to withdraw land from production. Altogether, these measures will cut farm spending from 62 percent in 1988 to 56 percent of the total EC budget by 1992.

Despite these reforms, the EC has balked at more far-reaching proposals by the U.S. and others to begin to move toward multilateral elimination of agricultural subsidies by 2000. The troubled Uruguay Round of GATT negotiations demonstrate that Europe's 10 million farmers remain a very powerful and effective political lobby.

---

13 Hitiris, 1988, p. 135.

14 European Commission, "Annual Economic Report," 1989, p. 265; Hitiris, 1988, p. 128; and *Agricultural Outlook*, 1990, p. 29.

15 Demekas et al., 1988, p. 140.

The CAP is seen by some as the necessary price for overall freer trade. It creates a constituency in every member country in support of the EC. North America may need to find its own glue for its common market (freer immigration, perhaps). Hopefully, it will not be such expensive glue. The CAP demonstrates that common market institutions do not necessarily lead to an expansion in state aid as much as an absorption of previous support policies from the member governments. In fact, the creation of a community may make instituting protectionism more difficult because there are more parties to convince. Nevertheless, the community remains vulnerable to the same internal protectionist pressures. Once a community institutionalizes the framework for sectoral protectionism, such as CAP, it will have a very difficult time unravelling it.

Tax Policy

The EC's tax policy has proved to be one of the most controversial issues in the community. While all the member states agree on the need for some approximation of rates for the single internal market, they do not agree on how to achieve this goal. Each country sees the power to tax as central to its national sovereignty and each worries about the loss of revenue or loss of business that could occur with an EC-wide system.

Tax policy is complicated by the wide variation between member states in terms of rates and structure. For example, although Denmark has only one value-added tax (VAT) rate, Belgium has five. Rates range from an average of 12 percent in Luxembourg and Spain to an average of 25 percent in Ireland. For this reason, a BMW in Germany costs $17,500 U.S. while one in Greece costs $50,000 U.S. With respect to excise taxes, countries tax similar products, but levy vastly different rates. Northern countries tax alcohol and tobacco heavily for health and safety reasons; southern countries tax them lightly to support local industry. Direct taxes also vary, though not as widely as they once did. Corporate tax rates range from 35 percent in the United Kingdom and Spain to 50 percent in Germany. The highest marginal income tax rates on individuals range from 40 percent in the U.K. and Portugal to 68 percent in Denmark.

The harmonization of EC members' tax systems promises to be a complicated and extended project. The earliest EC proposals could possibly be fully implemented is 1996. Nevertheless, the competitive pressures of free moving capital, labour, and goods will continue to force considerable informal convergence of rates. Countries with moderate tax rates and reasonable, predictable regulations will win business and attract investment capital from countries with high tax rates and burdensome, capricious regulations.

International competition to hold down the cost of government is likely to prove more effective than centrally planned harmonization. In the 1980s, the highest income tax rates were significantly reduced in every Western European nation except Switzerland (which already had the lowest tax rates, see table 1). Yet Belgium was one of the last nations to reduce marginal tax rates at the end of the 1980s, along with The Netherlands and West Germany. Had these decisions been dominated by a Belgian EC bureaucracy, instead of by competition for human and financial capital, attempts might instead have been made to harmonize tax rates in an upward direction.

As the experience of the U.S. shows, it is not really necessary for each member of a common market to have identical tax structures. Some American states have no income tax, some exclude clothing or food from the sales tax. Competition, though, did force New York to bring tax rates closer to those of New Jersey, and Quebec to bring tax rates down toward those of Ontario.

It is likewise not at all necessary to have central supervision of European budget deficits in order to make a European monetary union work. Several countries with very large, chronic budget deficits, such as The Netherlands and Belgium, have long maintained extremely strong currencies. Countries with sustained budget surpluses—Britain, Sweden, Australia, and Denmark—have frequently used deliberate currency devaluation in a futile effort to gain some trade or employment objective. Indeed, the EMS has worked as well as it has precisely because it limits the scope of co-ordination to central banking, rather than wrangling over budgets or trade, as the G-7 nations often do.

Table 1
Maximum Marginal Tax Rates
on Individual Income

	1979	1990
Belgium	76%	55%
Denmark	73%	68%
France	60%	53%
West Germany	56%	53%
Greece	60%	50%
Ireland	65%	56%
Italy	72%	50%
The Netherlands	72%	60%
Portugal	84%	40%
Spain	66%	56%
U.K.	83%	40%

Source: Price Waterhouse; International Bureau of Fiscal Documentation.

Social Policy

Included in the 1992 agenda is a social action program which involves 47 measures addressing workers' rights. The EC Council has already adopted three directives which include a regulation on how much a manual worker can carry and one mandating free eye exams for those who work with visual display units. The Council is currently debating three more measures, recently approved by the Commission; 14 weeks paid maternity leave, limited work hours for overtime and night employees, and mandated social benefits for part-time workers employed for more than eight hours a week. Other proposals to be considered are a common minimum wage (sure to cause unemployment in low productivity economies) and worker representation on company boards.

While some social program measures will undoubtedly pass since similar provisions are already in effect throughout the EC, others face a difficult battle in the Council of Ministers. The U.K. has consistently opposed proposals to impose costly, mandated wages and benefits and could block any directive addressing employment concerns which require unanimous consent. Health and safety regulations, on the other hand, could pass more easily because they only require a majority vote.

External Trade Relations

Anxiety about a "Fortress Europe," with formidable tariffs or quotas on non-EC goods, is most acute in the auto, textile, and computer industries. As with agriculture, though, the likely risk is not that new trade barriers will go up, but that old national barriers will not go down. Imports of Japanese cars are already limited to 3 percent of the market in France and 1 percent in Italy. In 1990 Japanese cars accounted for about 10 percent of Europe's market of 13.5 million autos, while Ford and GM accounted for 23 percent.[16] The U.S. brands are mostly from European plants, but Japanese cars are being manufactured in Britain, while Volvo and Daimler Benz are discussing joint ventures with Mitsubishi. In North America the Honda Accord has 75 percent U.S. content; the Ford Probe LX is built in Michigan by Mazda (which is 25 percent owned by Ford) and has a U.S. engine; the Geo Tracker is a Suzuki made in Canada; the Mercury Tracer is a Ford-Mazda hybrid from Mexico; and the Mercury Capri is a Ford-Mazda from Australia. Even if Europe thought it could safely impose "voluntary export restraints" on Japan, it would be far more risky to try that with Japanese joint ventures from North America, and seemingly impossible with Japanese cars from Britain. Competition is as unavoidable for Renault, Fiat, and Volkswagen as it was for the late unlamented East German Trabant.

16 Marcam, 1990.

In computers Europe's industry is too dependent on Asian components to get overly abrasive in trade relations, and the U.S. is at least equally tough competition in this industry. If the EC could somehow protect companies that produced overpriced or inferior computers, that would cripple thousands of computer-dependent European industries. In today's increasingly informed and open world markets, the European buyers' interest in abundance, variety, and low prices is likely to outweigh some sellers' interest in scarcity, cartels, and high prices.

There is a commonly expressed anxiety about the world soon becoming divided into three trading blocs—Europe, Asia, and North America—with freer internal trade, but increased external protectionism. Yet there is no obvious reason why the beneficial experience of reduced protectionism among any group of countries should make them more protectionist toward other countries. The expanding list of EC countries, for example, share no common interest in restricting the imports of, say, North American autos. Many EC countries do not even produce autos. Other EC countries have substantial investments at stake in numerous North American export industries, as well as joint ventures with Asian industries.

A combined North America would likewise have no less interest than it always has had in exporting to Europe and Asia, and therefore could not be indifferent toward retaliation for any "Fortress America" behaviour. Also, newly-revived economies such as Mexico and Chile have experienced the benefits (lower costs) of unilateral reduction of their once-formidable tariffs and import quotas. This now opens the way for further reciprocal reductions of serious trade barriers that industrial countries still place against Third World farm products and textiles. If one bloc, say the EC, remained protectionist against such developing countries, while an Asian and/or North American bloc did not, the protectionist bloc would find itself facing both higher costs for protected products and reduced trade with the most promising emerging economies of the Third World (who naturally tend to import where they can export).

Any trade bloc centred around Japan and Asian NICs would remain a huge net importer of food, raw materials, and services, while North America is a vital exporter in these areas. The only contemporary examples of genuinely autarkic trade blocs—the Soviet Union and Comecon—are obviously eager to open up trade outside the bloc, despite some unfortunate Balkanization of internal trade among the Soviet states. This is the opposite pattern from that predicted by those concerned that free trade zones will somehow feel so self-sufficient that they will close themselves off to external trade, as Comecon once did.

The rise of new EC-like organizations to negotiate freer trade within North America and Asia is a net reduction in existing trade barriers, not something that need replace broader negotiations for free trade within GATT, the OECD, the IMF, G-7, etc. The movement toward regional common markets is part of a clear trend toward opening up world markets for capital, goods, and services. Fortress walls are coming down, world-wide, not going up.

Estimated Benefits of the European Common Market

The benefits of a common market potentially encompass a variety of economic and political impacts.

Economic Impacts

The Cecchini Report, a study commissioned by the EC, estimates that Europe's 1992 program could bring a one-time real increase in Europe's GDP (base year, 1988) that would eventually amount to 5 to 7 percent, a 4 to 6 percent reduction in the level of consumer prices, and two to five million additional jobs.[17] Professor Richard Baldwin of Columbia University, among others, has argued that these results underestimate the benefits of the EC 1992 project by 450 percent because they ignore the impact on the long-run trajectory of growth. While Cecchini based his estimates solely on the one-time gain of a more efficient use of resources, Baldwin took into account a full range of dynamic effects arising from expanded opportunities and increased market size. These include greater innovation, accelerated sharing of technologies and ideas, more investment, improved productivity gains, and resulting higher output growth. He concluded that permanently higher investment and innovation rates after 1992 could raise the EC's annual growth rate by a total of 0.2 to 0.9 percent year after year, with a consequent boost to GDP levels of 11 to 35 percent.[18]

Early economic indicators from 1988 to 1990 already suggest that Cecchini and others may have underestimated the gains to Europe. Real growth in EC GDP for 1988 and 1989 were 4.1 percent and 3.6 percent, respectively, after eight years of growth rates below 2.7 percent, and this improvement continued in the first quarter of 1990. The Gulf Crisis and a possible U.S.-Canadian recession damaged short-term growth prospects in Europe (and vice versa for North America), but the EC now appears much more capable of handling these economic threats than they were just a decade ago.

The economic benefits from EC integration now look larger than expected for several reasons:

17 Cecchini et al., 1988, p. 101. The U.S. Congressional Budget Office model predicts that integration will raise Europe's real GNP by 5.4 to 6.2 percent by the year 2000, and will also raise U.S. real GNP very slightly by 0.1 to 0.2 percent. See Congressional Budget Office, 1990, p. xv.

18 Baldwin, 1989, p. 269. See also Barro and Romer, 1990.

- **Trade creation.** Despite early anxieties to the contrary, the trade creation effects of an EC customs union appear to far exceed trade diversion (where goods from within the bloc substitute for lower cost goods outside the bloc, solely because of preferential tariffs and quotas). This means that outside countries like the U.S. will benefit more from growth opportunities in the EC than they will lose from trade diverted to other EC countries. Experts estimate trade creation effects to outweigh diversion between five- and ten-fold.[19]

- **Efficiency gains.** The gains in efficiency from more intense competition have turned out to be far more critical than the direct trade gains. These include improved economies of scale, lower prices in formerly protected markets for inputs, and increased entrepreneurial innovation and investment. As Michael Emerson, senior economist at the Commission notes, "the resource cost of frontiers is peanuts," compared with distortions caused by restricted entry into markets.[20] These efficiency gains have been underestimated in the past because earlier economic analyses, which were based on static models, ignored the dynamic effects.

- **Confidence gains.** No one anticipated the remarkable speed at which business and world investors would embrace the integration project. Benefits have begun to be realized even before 1992 reforms are implemented, as companies anticipate the event. In 1988, for example, capital investment in the EC grew by 9 percent—more than double the consensus forecasts. Foreign direct and equity investment into the EC in 1988-1990 was often described as "euphoric," before the Mideast uncertainties put plans on hold.

Safeguards for Smaller Countries

Overall, less affluent countries have found membership in the EC particularly rewarding. That none of these countries even remotely contemplates leaving the union attests to its success. People have begun to proclaim a Spanish and Portuguese miracle after seeing the high growth and lower inflation rates since their membership to the EC. (See table 2). Economic integration brings an investment boom as business confidence improves. It keeps inflation down by requiring closer monetary co-ordination. It creates opportunities that reward those who invest in education and punish those who overstaff.

19 Bieber et al., 1988, p. 37. Also see Hufbauer, 1990, p. 22.
20 Colchester, 1990, p. 15.

Table 2
Economic Indicators for Spain and Portugal Before
and After Membership to the EC in 1986

	GDP Growth		Inflation	
	1983-1986	1986-1988	1983-1986	1986-1988
Portugal	1.7%	4.6%	22.3%	11.4%
Spain	2.5%	5.2%	10.1%	5.8%

Source: OECD National Accounts, Paris 1990.

However, integration alone cannot guarantee that less affluent countries will grow fast enough to catch up with the more prosperous EC countries. Just as important is a general environment of strong economic growth. Although regional disparities declined during the early period of EC integration, they increased with the economic difficulties of the late 1970s and early 1980s. Also critical is the implementation of the appropriate government policies. Spain and Portugal have been able to reap great rewards from integration because both countries have made credible and comprehensive changes in policy ranging from privatization to more stable monetary policies. On the other hand, the economic records of Greece and Ireland have been mixed. Ireland, which joined the EC in 1973, only recently began to record a strong and steady growth rate since its fiscal adjustment program was implemented in 1985. Greece, currently outside of the ERM, has the highest inflation rate and one of the fastest growth rates for government consumption in the EC. Its GDP per capita actually fell relative to the EC average from 58 percent in 1980 to 51 percent in 1989.

To help incorporate economically diverse members into one community, the EC relies on transition periods and structural assistance for less affluent countries. The community has more than doubled its regional development fund over the past ten years to 4.7 billion ECU's (roughly $6.5 billion).

It also has developed institutional arrangements such as qualified majority voting to give smaller powers a louder voice. Qualified majority voting, which applies to all issues except those critical to national sovereignty such as taxation and immigration, distributes votes among countries depending on their size and importance in the EC. Britain, France, Italy, and Germany have ten votes. Spain has eight. Belgium, Greece, Holland, and Portugal have five. Denmark and Ireland have three and Luxembourg has two. The system is carefully constructed so that three larger countries must act as a block to veto any legislation. The smaller countries, acting as a group, are also powerful enough to stop a decision.

Political Impacts

Success at economic integration has spilled over into the political realm, building goodwill among the members, and improving the EC's effectiveness in serving as a common voice on global issues. Better political relations have developed simply because the different countries have more contact with each other and because they have developed a common interest based on lower barriers and increased trade.

The establishment of the EC has brought its member countries more political clout in international affairs. In 1980 the EC effectively undermined President Carter's grain embargo against the Soviet Union, agreeing only to limit subsidies on EC grain sales that would substitute for U.S. sales. In 1982 the EC took an even more vocal approach, vehemently denouncing President Reagan's embargo of vital components for a Soviet-Europe pipeline. These positions helped the EC financially and politically. They demonstrated an ability to act as a unified and distinct voice, effectively circumventing U.S. power. Evidence of the EC's success can be seen in the large number of countries seeking membership. Sweden, Austria, Malta, Cyprus, and Turkey want to become members now. Norway, Finland, and Switzerland want to become members soon. Even Eastern Europe eagerly waits in line.

The EC also capably demonstrates how a community may have to bend the rules to accommodate special interest pressure groups. Using various creative mechanisms, it has permitted side agreements which excepted vulnerable industries or sectors from overall EC mandates for lower barriers. The European Coal and Steel Community (ECSC), which still operates today, offers an important example. Its governing body limits imports, sets production levels, and controls prices for all EC countries. The CAP offers another. Agricultural assistance has been instrumental in building unified support for the EC among farmers across many countries. Both programs have been used to buy off opposition—by industrial sector, not country. Obviously, too many such exceptions could violate the liberalizing rule. Alternatively, the EC eases the restructuring process through retraining support, infrastructure projects, and grants or loans for high-growth industries.

Estimated Benefits of a North American Common Market

Economic Impacts

North America can use the EC experience as a starting point for evaluating the benefits of its own community. For several reasons, a North American common market would surely produce even larger economic gains for its participants than the EC could for its members. First, the barriers within North America are substantially greater than within pre-1992 Europe, in spite of the Canada-U.S.

Free Trade Agreement and substantial unilateral tariff reduction in Mexico. Some of the most destructive barriers include state aid to business, government procurement, financial services, and labour mobility (in both directions—Mexico is highly restrictive toward needed foreign specialists). Greater barriers mean greater benefits when they are dismantled.

Second, trade between Mexico, Canada, and the United States is complementary. The U.S. would benefit from improved access to the large natural resources base in Canada and Mexico as well as Mexico's expanding and increasingly skilled labour base. Mexico and Canada would benefit from better access to U.S. capital resources, technical know-how, and sophisticated service sector. Companies operating in Canada and Mexico will achieve economies of scale with improved access to the much larger U.S. market with its population of 248 million. In every country, competition and information will increase as import penetration rises.

Growth estimates will need to be adjusted to account for the different levels and types of barriers at work. In some ways, a NACM could be more beneficial than the EC because North America faces the additional hurdle of divergent standards and regulations across the states and provinces within the three member countries. For example, the EC allows physicians, engineers, and architects (though not lawyers) to transfer professional qualifications from one country to another. The U.S., on the other hand, has individual state regulations on 740 different professions.[21] The EC has introduced a product liability directive which will create a more uniform standard throughout Europe. The U.S. continues to maintain 50 different laws regulating business.

At first glance, the benefits of a NACM may appear relatively modest, because trade among the dozen EC countries reached $660 billion in 1989, while trade between the three North American economies was only $165 billion. But there are two problems with that comparison. First, the existing level of trade between North American countries, which still maintain significant tariffs and import quotas against each other, says virtually nothing about what potential trade could be in the absence of those trade barriers. Second, trade between France and Italy is not fundamentally different than trade between New York and New Jersey, or between British Columbia and Alberta. If the EC's dozen countries had already combined into three common markets, as the federations of the U.S., Mexico, and Canada had, then nobody would even bother to measure trade between those 12 "nations"—any more than anyone pays much attention to trade between U.S. cities or states. The objective of economic union is the increased production of what consumers want to buy

---

21 Pelkmans et al., 1988, p. 82.

at the lowest possible cost, *not* maximizing the amount of merchandise crossing arbitrary borders.

Distribution of Costs and Benefits

Like North America, the EC countries have been concerned with the regional distribution of costs and benefits from closer economic union. However, EC experience demonstrates that integration does not necessarily imply a sudden, large move of manufacturing activities to regions with a comparative cost advantage or a flood of immigrants to the more affluent countries. The decision of where to locate manufacturing facilities depends on much more than relative wage costs, including such factors as transportation costs and economies of scale. In fact, while Spain had the highest average growth rate in manufacturing employment over the past seven years, three of the wealthiest EC countries, Denmark, The Netherlands, and Germany, followed right behind. In 1989 every EC country recorded gains in manufacturing employment. A NACM will bring more foreign investment to Mexico from Canada and the U.S., but not necessarily at the expense of growth in manufacturing in the Northern countries. As in the EC, economic integration offers significant growth opportunities to all countries as trade increases and diversifies.

With respect to migration, the EC has found no wide-scale movement of people from the peripheral, poorer regions to the central, more affluent ones, despite significant differences in income level with countries like Greece and parts of Italy. Only Ireland reports net emigration, mostly to the U.K., continuing its historical pattern. Likewise, demographers do not expect a massive migration from Portugal and Spain when their restrictions are phased out in 1993.[22] If the EC experience is any indication, Mexicans will continue to migrate north at the same rate that they do now. However, given recent evidence that absolute wages more than relative wages spur migration, migration should slow as the Mexican economy improves.

A NACM offers less-advantaged regions the chance to signal a change in government approach. This is what Spain and Portugal have capitalized on to attract foreign investors. Together, with new policies to allow markets to work more efficiently, these countries have raised expectations, a component that can be as essential as the policies themselves to overall growth prospects. Mexico's efforts to grow fast enough to catch up with its more affluent northern neighbours will be solidified with the credibility that a NACM and its outside constraints provide.

---

22 Commission of the European Communities, 1990, p. 221.

Political Impacts

Integration ensures that countries have a forum to express their opinions toward the national decisions of others and perhaps influence decisions that most effect them. For Canada and Mexico, a NACM would eliminate the threat of unilateral trade retaliation by the U.S. under Super 301 provision of the 1988 Omnibus Trade and Competitiveness Act. For the U.S., a NACM would eliminate the threat of energy supply cut-offs as occurred in the 1970s by Canada and Mexico.

All three countries would benefit from the political goodwill that association brings. The NACM could provide the framework needed for Mexico, Canada, and the U.S. to reach common ground on such contentious issues as acid rain, fish resources, drugs, immigration, and debt.

Rather than leading to the domination of one country over another, integration can act as a safeguard to protect smaller countries. It was an integrated Europe that made possible and acceptable the unification of East and West Germany, precisely because membership in the EC acts as a constraining influence. Far from encroaching on distinct cultural identities, the development of the EC has allowed differences based on region and sector to flourish. Likewise in North America, connections between Houston and Monterrey and Toronto and Buffalo, artificially stifled now, will thrive under a NACM. In fact, these cross-border coalitions or sub-economies will become among the most vocal supporters of integration.

Relevance to North America

A North American common market would resemble the European Community in size. In terms of population, a NACM would contain 357 million people, while the EC holds 324 million. In terms of gross domestic product, a NACM would have reported $5,516 billion in 1988, while the EC reported $4,060 billion.[23]

Both entities must contend with significant regional disparities among and within member countries. Europe's poorest and richest members are as diverse as Portugal, with a per capita gross national product (GNP) of $3,650, and Luxembourg, with $22,400. The NACM's poorest and richest countries would be Mexico, with a per capita GNP of $1,760, and the U.S. with $19,840.[24] The per capita gap between the U.S. and Mexico appears substantially larger than the gap between Luxembourg and Portugal when expressed in U.S. dollars. Using World Bank data, though, Portugal still had a lower per capita GNP than Mexico as recently as 1985—$1,970 for Portugal, $2,080 for Mexico. By 1988,

23 The Central Intelligence Agency, 1989.

24 The World Bank, 1990. Figures are not adjusted for purchasing power parity, which makes Luxembourg appear more affluent than the U.S.

due to the sharp recovery of EC currencies against the dollar, Portugal's per capita GNP appeared to jump to $3,650. Obviously, though, the Portuguese people did not double their living standards in only three years! Converting Mexico's peso incomes into dollars likewise makes it look as though per capita GNP fell by 6.1 percent per year in this same period, from $2,080 to $1,760, even though Mexico's real GNP roughly kept pace with population growth, except in 1986 when GNP was deflated by Mexican prices. In short, the apparently greater income disparity between North America and Europe is largely a statistical illusion, due to unusual exchange rate fluctuations that do not properly measure actual purchasing power of Mexican and Portuguese incomes.

A NACM would differ in several fundamental ways from the EC. First, and most obviously, a NACM would encompass fewer states—three rather than 12. That would mean fewer languages, fewer religious, cultural, and political differences, and fewer negotiating parties to convince. Moreover, North America has fewer potential members (although President Bush has spoken of embracing all of Latin America). With the EC, expansion has always been a controversial issue. A wider community has hampered progress for a deeper community as new applications divert attention from the toughest integration issues and more members complicate the decision process.

Second, while Europe's ultimate objective has always included some degree of political unification, a NACM does not. Consequently, North America could have an easier time defining its agenda and accomplishing its goals. As Europe discovered early, progress on the economic front comes much more quickly than progress in forging a common defence policy or a common social policy (for example, a single minimum wage).

Third, North America is clearly dominated by the United States, in terms of economic position, political clout, and population. While the European Community contains Germany, an economic powerhouse, Germany's influence is reduced because of the 11 other members. Germany shares equal voting power with France, Italy, and Great Britain. The relative power imbalance in North America could make negotiations more difficult for the United States as sovereignty concerns on the part of Mexico and Canada overwhelm discussion, or it could make negotiations easier if the U.S. uses its support and influence to smooth the transition.

Fourth, the issue of monetary union is not so troublesome as it has been between Britain and Germany. Mexico has been explicitly adapting its monetary policy toward a fixed parity with the U.S. dollar by gradually slowing the "crawling peg" slippage of the peso.[25] Canada also rarely lets its currency swing

25 Reynolds et al., 1990, chapter 8.

very far from the U.S. dollar. The only seeming "benefit" from retaining the sovereign right to devalue the Canadian dollar is that Canadian interest rates are always higher than in the U.S., even when current inflation is similar. Canada's higher interest rates apparently include a risk premium against an unnecessary uncertainty about exchange rate losses. A greater degree of monetary union within North America should not present greater difficulties, though the relationship to the ECU and yen, and an "anchor" to real commodities, remains a global challenge.

Despite these differences, North America has much to learn from Europe. The EC experience demonstrates how to set both realistic yet courageous and inspirational goals for economic union. It shows the value of building a union through modest, lasting steps which take care not to unnecessarily or prematurely step on national sovereignty. It offers a showcase of unique approaches to inevitable problems that a NACM will face. Most important, it emphasizes that economic integration, which tackles the most serious impediments whether mutual recognition of standards or the right to work in any country, is feasible and indeed worthwhile.

References

Agricultural Outlook, "Europe in Turmoil," May 1990.

Baldwin, Richard, "The Growth Effects of 1992," *Economic Policy*, October 1989.

Barro, Robert, and Paul Romer, "Economic Growth," *NBER Reporter*, Cambridge, Mass.: National Bureau of Economic Research, Fall 1990.

Betts, Paul, "EC Considers Third Stage to Open up Air Transport," *Financial Times*, August 29, 1990.

Bieber, Roland, et al., *1992: One European Market? A Critical Analysis of the Commission's Internal Market Strategy*, Baden-Baden: Nomos Verlagsgesellschaft, 1988.

Cecchini, Paolo, et al., *The European Challenge, 1992*, Brookfield, Vt.: Gower Publishing Company, 1988.

The Central Intelligence Agency, *Handbook of Economic Statistics*, Washington, D.C.: Government Printing Office, 1989.

Colchester, Nicholas, "Europe's Internal Market Survey," *The Economist*, July 9, 1990.

Commission of the European Communities, "One Market, One Money: An evaluation of the potential benefits and costs of forming an economic and monetary union," *European Economy*, No. 44, October 1990.

Congressional Budget Office, *How the Economic Transformations in Europe Will Affect the United States*, Washington, D.C.: The Congress of the United States, December 1990.

Demekas, Dimitrios, et al., "The Effects of the Common Agricultural Policy of the European Community; A Survey of the Literature," *Journal of Common Market Studies*, December 1988.

Drouin, Marie-Josee, Maurice Ernst, and Jimmy W. Wheeler, *Western European Adjustment to Structural Economic Problems*, Indianapolis: Hudson Institute, 1987.

European Commission, "Annual Economic Report," *European Economy*, No. 42, November 1989.

European Commission, "Europe Without Frontiers: a Review Half-way to 1992," *European File*, Luxembourg: Office for Official Publications of the European Communities, June-July 1989.

European Commission, *Second Survey on State Aids in the European Community*, Luxembourg: Office for Official Publications of the European Communities, 1990.

European Commission, *Target 92*, No. 5-1990, Luxembourg: Office for Official Publications of the European Communities, 1990.

EC Bulletin, "Completion of Internal Market Statistics," August 31, 1990.

Hitiris, T., *European Community Economics*, New York: Simon & Schuster International Group, 1988.

Hoffman, Stanley, "The European Communities and 1992," *Foreign Affairs*, Vol. 68, Fall 1989.

Hufbauer, Gary Clyde, ed., *Europe 1992; An American Perspective*, Washington D.C.: Brookings Institution, 1990.

Marcam, John, Jr., "The Unacceptable Face of Protectionism," *Forbes*, November 12, 1990.

McDonald, Frank, and George Zis, "The European Monetary System: Towards 1992 and Beyond," *Journal of Common Market Studies*, No. 3, March 1989.

Pelkmans, Jacques, et al., *The Internal Markets of North America*, Luxembourg: Office for Official Publications of the European Communities, 1988.

Reynolds, Alan, et al., "Theory behind Devaluation and Austerity," *Mexico 2000*, Morristown, N.J.: Polyconomics Inc., 1990.

Swann, Dennis, *The Economics of a Common Market*, London: Penguin Books, 1990.

Ungerer, Horst, Owen Evans, Thomas Mayer, and Philip Young, "The European Monetary System: Recent Developments," *IMF Occasional Paper No. 48*, Washington D.C.: IMF, 1986.

U.S. Department of Commerce, *EC 1992: A Commerce Department Analysis of European Community Directives Vol. 3*, March 1990.

The World Bank, *World Development Report*, New York: Oxford University Press, 1990.

Appendix

A Perspective on Trilateral Economic Relations

Steven Globerman and Maureen Bader

The purpose of this appendix is to outline in broad terms the current status of trilateral economic relations. An overview of current trade and investment relations should be useful background to the discussion contained in the various chapters of the text. It also helps put into perspective the scope for closer economic relations between Canada, Mexico, and the United States in the future.

Trade Relations

Both the Canadian and Mexican economies are closely tied through trade to the U.S. economy. The magnitude of these ties is illustrated by tables 1 and 2. As shown in table 1, Canada exported almost $98 billion (Canadian) of merchandise to the U.S. in 1989. This represented more than 73 percent of all Canadian merchandise exports in that year. Canadian merchandise imports from the U.S. approached $88 billion in 1989 or approximately 65 percent of all Canadian merchandise imports in that same year.

As table 2 indicates, Mexico also trades heavily with the United States. For example, Mexico exported around $23 billion (U.S.) of merchandise to the U.S. in 1988 and imported about $21 billion from the U.S. This represented about 65 percent of Mexico's merchandise exports and imports for that year.

The U.S. economy is more diversified than either Canada's or Mexico's in terms of the geographic sourcing of its exports and imports. For example, imports from its largest trading partner, Canada, amounted to somewhat less than 20 percent of all U.S. merchandise imports in 1987, while exports to Canada were less than 25 percent of all U.S. merchandise exports in the same year. The latter are significant percentages none-the-less. By comparison, U.S.

Table 1
Canadian Merchandise Trade with the United States
(Thousands of Canadian Dollars)

	1988		1989	
	Exports	Imports	Exports	Imports
Food and live animals	3,905,533	3,815,036	3,906,107	3,799,757
Beverages and tobacco	507,061	507,061	483,921	483,921
Crude materials, inedible, exc. fuel	1,224,051	1,089,053	1,202,346	1,082,510
Mineral fuels, lubricants, related matr.	10,212,588	1,637,801	10,283,179	2,015,345
Oils and fats, animal & vegetable	105,592	90,497	92,386	106,350
Chemicals and related products	4,026,639	4,225,446	3,908,337	4,682,458
Manufactured goods by chief material	30,065,452	17,303,184	28,593,063	18,441,842
Machinery and transport equipment	44,829,089	52,404,949	45,615,459	51,324,466
Miscellaneous mfrd. artcls, nspf	2,021,131	3,861,908	2,128,079	4,468,576
Articles not provided for elsewhere	633,252	1,814,237	1,672,101	1,784,491
Total	97,530,434	86,020,888	97,930,006	87,914,295

Source: Hart, 1990, table 11.

Table 2
Mexican Merchandise Trade with the United States
(Thousands of U.S.dollars)

	1987		1988	
	Exports	Imports	Exports	Imports
Food and live animals	2,072,492	670,137	1,927,264	1,517,245
Beverages and tobacco	270,981	11,563	264,525	22,469
Crude materials, inedible, exc. fuel	276,165	1,049,957	368,846	1,464,790
Mineral fuels, lubricants, related matr.	3,856,901	510,256	3,314,478	458,034
Oils and fats, animal & vegetable	3,705	95,363	8,330	142,023
Chemicals and related products	507,055	1,450,862	724,466	1,833,657
Manufactured goods by chief material	2,006,895	1,541,672	2,466,126	2,262,185
Machinery and transport equipment	8,727,248	7,333,203	10,928,273	10,089,075
Miscellaneous mfrd. artcls, nspf	1,776,571	1,337,181	2,279,395	1,983,279
Articles not provided for elsewhere	772,773	569,361	995,187	860,505
Total	20,270,785	14,569,554	23,276,890	20,633,263

Source: Hart, 1990, table 8.

imports from Mexico were around 5 percent of all U.S. merchandise imports in 1987, while exports to Mexico constituted around 6 percent of all U.S. merchandise exports in the same year.

To date, the amount of direct trade between Mexico and Canada is relatively small, as shown in table 3. For example, Canada exported around $600 million (Canadian) to Mexico in 1989 and imported approximately $1.7 billion of merchandise from Mexico. These amount to around 0.5 percent and 1.3 percent of total Canadian merchandise exports and imports, respectively. These trade estimates are undoubtedly understated, however, given an unknown volume of merchandise that is transhipped through the U.S. It is also relevant to note that trade between Mexico and Canada has grown relatively quickly in the past few years.

The major traded manufactured goods in the North American context are identified in tables 4 through 9. Specifically, tables 4 and 5 report Canada's major manufactured exports to the U.S. and Mexico, respectively. Tables 6 and 7 report Mexico's major manufactured exports to the U.S. and Canada, respectively, and tables 8 and 9 report the main U.S. manufactured exports to Canada and Mexico.

Several observations from these tables are worth highlighting. One is the prominence of the motor vehicle industry in North American trade. Assembled motor vehicles and motor vehicle parts and accessories are the single largest category of U.S.-Canada bilateral trade in manufactured goods. Moreover, next to petroleum exports, motor vehicles combined with motor vehicle parts and accessories constitute Mexico's largest manufactured export category to the U.S., while motor vehicle parts and accessories are Mexico's largest category of manufactured exports to Canada. Quite clearly, the impact of trilateral economic integration on the motor vehicle industry is of great relevance to the overall economic consequences of closer economic relations among the three countries; however, the substantial amount of trilateral trade in agricultural products (not shown in the tables) and chemical products should also be noted, as should Mexico's exports of mineral fuel products to the U.S. and Canada's exports of forest and metal products.

Table 3
Canadian Merchandise Trade with Mexico
(Thousands of Canadian Dollars)

	1988		1989	
	Exports	Imports	Exports	Imports
Food and live animals	157,845	112,206	150,336	112,354
Beverages and tobacco	307	12,596	223	15,363
Crude materials, inedible, exc. fuel	48,547	69,172	45,220	23,295
Mineral fuels, lubricants, related matr.	2,886	59,753	38	49,406
Oils and fats, animal & vegetable	1,827	—	1,741	—
Chemicals and related products	18,872	13,505	7,668	13,845
Manufactured goods by chief material	117,261	191,064	161,829	332,104
Machinery and transport equipment	129,798	828,706	213,830	1,100,863
Miscellaneous mfrd. artcls, nspf	3,954	29,965	4,769	42,381
Articles not provided for elsewhere	7,662	10,716	17,397	8,718
Total	489,002	1,327,726	603,098	1,698,368

Source: Hart, 1990, table 9.

Table 4
Canada's Major Manufactured Exports to the U.S., 1987

	Major SIC Group	($000's Canadian)	Percentage of Total Manufactured Exports
322 -	Motor vehicles	14,374,123	18.5
325 -	Motor vehicle parts & accessories	11,162,825	14.4
324 -	Truck, busbodies	5,963,370	7.7
27 -	Paper and allied products	9,070,761	11.7
25 -	Wood products	5,165,548	6.7
29 -	Primary metals	5,324,514	6.9
30 -	Fabricated metals	4,016,238	5.2
	Grand total	77,708,935	

Note: The grand totals reported in tables 4-9 include a residual category which is not explicitly shown in any of the tables. This is also why the percentages in the second columns fail to equal 100.

Source: Statistics Canada, Catalogue 65-003.

Table 5

Canada's Major Manufactured Exports to Mexico, 1987

	Major SIC Group	($000's Canadian)	Percentage of Total Manufactured Exports
35 -	Non-metallic minerals	72,944	18.4
325 -	Motor vehicle parts & accessories	63,256	15.9
30 -	Fabricated metals	64,343	16.2
31 -	Machinery	55,328	13.9
27 -	Paper and allied products	42,056	10.6
	Grand total	397,206	

Source: Statistics Canada, Catalogue 65-003.

Table 6

Mexico's Major Manufactured Exports to the U.S., 1987

Major SIC Group	(000's U.S.)	Percentage of Total Manufactured Exports
319 - Other machinery & equipment	1,752,660	12.4
323 - Motor vehicles	1,176,444	8.3
36 - Refined petroleum and coal products	3,799,433	26.8
325 - Motor vehicle parts & accessories	667,550	4.7
11 - Food products	992,449	7.0
29 - Primary metals	680,030	4.8
Grand total	14,177,450	

Source: U.S. Bureau of Census, Highlights of U.S. Export and Import Trade (FT 990).

Table 7
Mexico's Major Manufactured Exports to Canada, 1987

	Major SIC Group	(000's Canadian)	Percentage of Total Manufactured Exports
325 -	Motor vehicle parts & accessories	535,925	59.4
323 -	Motor vehicles	61,609	6.8
336 -	Office machinery and equipment	72,152	8.0
335 -	Other telecommunications and related equipment	60,275	6.7
10 -	Food products	40,462	4.5
18 -	Primary textiles	34,088	3.8
	Grand total	902,152	

Source: Statistics Canada, Catalogue 65-003.

Table 8
U.S. Major Manufactured Exports to Canada, 1987

	Major SIC Group	(000's Canadian)	Percentage of Total Manufactured Exports
325 -	Motor vehicle parts and accessories	15,276,032	21.8
323 -	Motor vehicles	9,115,614	13.0
336 -	Office machinery and parts	4,472,723	6.4
319 -	Other machinery	6,101,689	8.7
37 -	Chemical products	3,087,888	4.4
30 -	Fabricated metals	3,722,620	5.3
	Grand total	69,974,100	

Source: Statistics Canada, Catalogue 65-003.

Table 9

U.S. Major Manufactured Exports to Mexico, 1987

	Major SIC Group	(000's U.S.)	Percentage of Total Manufactured Exports
37 -	Chemical products	1,391,227	14.4
325 -	Motor vehicle parts and accessories	1,307,440	13.6
319 -	Other machinery	1,991,014	20.7
27 -	Paper and allied products	610,393	6.3
10 -	Food products	555,219	5.8
335 -	Other telecommunications	500,722	5.2
	Grand total	9,641,300	

Source: U.S. Bureau of the Census (FT 990).

Trade Regimes

Besides the General Agreement on Tariffs and Trade (GATT), Canada-U.S. trade relations are largely governed by provisions of the Canada-U.S. Free Trade Agreement (FTA). It is not possible, nor necessarily advisable in this brief appendix to discuss the major provisions of the FTA in any detail; however, the main features of the FTA encompass the following items:

1. Provides for the elimination of all tariffs over a ten-year period beginning January 1, 1989;
2. Provides for each country to retain separate commercial policies for trade and economic relations with third countries;
3. Incorporates the fundamental national treatment obligation of the GATT which insures that once goods have been imported into either country, they will not be the object of discrimination; extends the principle of national treatment to the providers of a list of commercial services.
4. Implements a binding binational appeal process for anti-dumping and countervailing duty cases, as well as a binational review process governing changes in trade laws;
5. Incorporates an agreement between the two federal governments that the use of standards-related measures as unnecessary obstacles to trade will be avoided;
6. Retains basic provisions of the Canada-U.S. Auto Pact while providing that all vehicles traded under the FTA will be subject to a special rule of origin. Specifically, 50 percent of the direct production costs of any vehicle traded under the FTA will have to be incurred in Canada and the U.S. to qualify for duty-free treatment. The equivalent of a 70 percent share of overhead and other indirect costs are required as well to qualify for duty-free treatment;
7. Beyond a transition period and with some exceptions, neither country can implement emergency safeguards against imports from the other country without the other party's consent;
8. Provides for some deepening (beyond the GATT Code) for liberalizing government procurement;
9. Incorporates provisions that prohibit discriminatory taxes or charges on energy exports or to otherwise charge higher prices for such exports. Affirms a common interest in ensuring access to each other's markets;
10. Leaves general rules to deal with subsidies, dumping, and other unfair trade practices for later negotiations;
11. Retains supply management regimes and price support mechanisms for agricultural products;
12. Exempts the cultural and transportation sectors from the agreement.

Until fairly recently, Mexico stood largely outside the multilateral trading system; however, since the debt crisis of 1982, Mexico has dramatically reformed its trading regime. Fundamental trade liberalization began in 1983 and can be identified as having taken place in two stages: 1983 through mid-1985 and mid-1985 through 1989. Most important to the first stage were changes in tariffs, import licence requirements and official import prices. The accession to the GATT in 1986 and the U.S.-Mexico bilateral agreement in November 1987 mark important events in the second stage.

Tables 10 and 11 provide a brief overview of changes in tariffs and in import licensing. As table 10 suggests, the decrease in tariffs has been uneven over time. Indeed, tariffs actually increased in 1985 on a trade weighted basis, reflecting a countervailing force to the reduction in import licensing requirements and official import prices. Nevertheless, mean tariff rates tended to decline over the 1980s, so that by 1989, the trade weighted average tariff was close to 10 percent. This is not much higher than import duties were in Canada when that country began free trade discussions with the United States. By comparison, average U.S. tariffs are less than 5 percent. Tariff ranges in Mexico have also been significantly reduced, as suggested by the reduced dispersion of tariff rates reported in table 10. By the end of 1989, Mexico's tariff range was 0 to 20 percent. The GATT requires that its members stay within a range of 0 to 50 percent.

Another impediment to Mexican imports are official import reference prices. Any duty calculated is paid on the official reference price and not necessarily on the market value of the good. The official reference price was usually set substantially above the product's fair market value. The number of items subject to official reference prices has dropped considerably since 1983, and the import value of the relevant products is now an insignificant share of total Mexican imports.

The changes in import licence requirements began in July 1985 (see table 11). During the 1982 crisis, import licences were required for 100 percent of imports. After its accession to GATT, Mexico agreed to eliminate import licences (although some had been removed as early as 1984). Nevertheless, by December 1989 there were still licence requirements on 350 items including agricultural, chemical, and petrochemical products. Import duties were calculated on an item's official price rather than its transaction price. It was argued that these prices were necessary to combat dumping and export subsidies. Anti-dumping and countervailing duty laws were established in January 1986, and official import prices were no longer used after 1987.

Mexican trade liberalization continued in 1987 with a bilateral U.S.-Mexican agreement called the Framework of Principles and Procedures for Consultation Regarding Trade and Investment Relations. The "Framework" was an

Table 10
Import Tariff Structure

Year	Tariff Mean	Dispersion	Trade Weighted Av.	Number of Tariffs
1982	27.0	24.8	16.4	16
1983	23.8	23.5	8.2	13
1984	23.3	22.5	8.6	10
1985	25.5	18.8	13.3	10
1986	22.6	14.1	13.1	11
1987	10.0	6.9	5.6	5
1988	10.4	7.1	6.1	5
1989	13.1	4.3	9.8	5

Includes modifications in the tariff structure up to March 9, 1989.

Source: Zabludovsky, 1990, p. 195.

Table 11
Import Licensing in Mexico (1970-1988)

Year	Total Import Value	Controlled Import Value	Percentage Share
1970	2,328.3	1,590.2	68.3
1971	2,255.5	1,526.9	67.7
1972	2,762.1	1,831.2	66.3
1973	3,892.4	2,709.1	69.6
1974	6,148.6	5,041.8	82.0
1975	6,699.4	4,582.3	68.4
1976	2,299.9	5,695.1	90.4
1977	5,704.5	5,134.0	90.0
1978	7,917.5	6,041.1	76.3
1979	11,979.7	8,385.8	70.0
1980	18,896.6	11,337.9	60.0
1981	23,948.2	20,475.7	85.5
1982	14,437.0	14,437.0	100.0
1983	9,005.9	9,005.9	100.0
1984	11,254.5	9,397.3	83.5
1985	13,212.2	4,954.6	37.5
1986	11,432.4	3,532.6	30.9
1987	12,222.9	3,351.3	27.5
1988	18,777.0	3,699.1	19.7

Source: United States International Trade Commission, Publication 2278, pp. 4-5.

important step in the advancement of economic relations and understanding between Mexico and the United States. It highlighted the need to eliminate non-tariff barriers, the detrimental effects of protectionism, and the increased significance of services in both countries.

Before this agreement, there was no bilateral understanding between Mexico and the United States regarding commercial business. The "Framework" was followed by the signing of the Trade and Investment Facilitation Talks in October 1989. This agreement provided for a negotiating process. In February 1990 an understanding to further liberalize textile apparel trade was signed. Mexican exports of certain textiles and apparel are restricted by the multifibre arrangement. Previous to this, Mexico had extended its voluntary steel restraint program.

When Mexico acceded to the GATT, it was able to retain import licenses in three sectors: automobiles, electronics, and pharmaceuticals. The Mexican government is currently considering or is in the process of liberalizing its rules regarding all three sectors. Mexico's status as a Most Favoured Nation trading partner with the U.S. continues under the GATT, where the GATT largely replaced the traditional bilateral "friendship, commerce, and navigation" agreements that had been the principal means of establishing MFN treatment. As well, Mexico was designated as a beneficiary developing country in 1975 under the U.S. Generalized System of Preferences.

Prior to 1990, Canada and Mexico had signed several commercial agreements, but they had little impact on bilateral economic relations. However, in the first quarter of 1990, the Mexican and Canadian governments signed some ten separate agreements to promote economic exchange between the two countries, including a framework agreement to bolster trade and investment ties.

In summary, tariff reductions undertaken by the three countries under both the GATT and the FTA have largely eliminated tariffs as a significant obstacle to North American economic integration. As noted, the FTA will eliminate all tariffs between Canada and the U.S. before the turn of the century. The overwhelming majority of goods traded between Mexico and its North American partners is now duty free, and the tariffs on the residual items are for the most part relatively low. The major obstacles to closer economic integration on the trade regime side are the panoply of non-tariff barriers that exist under the relevant GATT provisions, as well as the FTA.

Foreign Investment and the Legislative Regime for Investing

Bilateral capital flows between Canada and the United States have been and continue to be relatively large. For example, by the end of 1985, Canadian direct investment assets in the U.S. had a book value of approximately $35.5 billion (Canadian) or around 14 percent of total foreign direct investment in the U.S.[1] From 1975 to 1985, Canadian direct investment in the U.S. grew by over 20 percent per year, and direct investment in the U.S. accounted for almost 60 percent of all Canadian direct investment abroad over this period.[2]

The book value of U.S. direct investments in Canada approached $63.5 billion (Canadian) at the end of 1985 having grown by around 7 percent per annum over the period 1975 to 1985. Direct investments in Canada accounted for approximately 17 percent of U.S. direct investment abroad in 1989.

Bilateral direct investment flows between Canada and the United States have been relatively unimpeded except in sectors designated as being reserved

1   See Rugman, 1987.
2   Ibid.

exclusively for domestically owned companies. In Canada the latter sectors include broadcasting, basic telecommunications, cable television, segments of the banking industry, and newspapers. The United States has a more limited coverage of so-called key sectors, most notably including broadcasting and sectors of the transportation industry; however, defence related businesses enjoy a measure of de facto domestic ownership requirements.

Under the FTA, the two governments agreed to extend the principle of national treatment to the providers of a list of commercial services. Excluding transportation, basic telecommunications, doctors, dentists, lawyers, child care, and government provided services (health, education, and social services), most commercial services are covered. This means that Canadian and American providers of these services must be treated identically in each country, although there is no necessary provision for each country to adopt the same domestic legislative regime governing the relevant businesses.

Canada continues to review eligible foreign direct investments under the Investment Canada Act. The act calls for review of new business investments and acquisitions of existing businesses above a certain size threshold to ensure that these investments provide net benefits for Canada. Under the FTA, U.S. investors are exempt from the review process for new investments but still must have acquisitions of Canadian businesses above a certain size reviewed by Investment Canada. The FTA provides that the review threshold for direct acquisitions will be raised in four steps to $150 million by 1992. It is estimated that at that time, about three-quarters of total non-financial assets in Canada now reviewable will still be reviewable. For indirect acquisitions, which involve the transfer of control of one foreign-controlled firm to another, the review process will be phased out over the same period; however, these changes to the Investment Canada review process will not apply to the oil and gas and uranium sectors.[3]

Mexico has historically taken a restrictive attitude towards inward direct investment; however, the 1982 debt crisis marked the beginning of a change in Mexico's attitude toward foreign direct investment (FDI), and significant liberalization has taken place since then. This is illustrated by the data in table 12 which show cumulative foreign direct investment in Mexico almost quadrupling between 1979 and 1989. U.S. companies were responsible for almost two-thirds of the cumulated investment by 1989. By contrast, Canada accounted for less than 2 percent of accumulated investment. Approximately two-thirds of all foreign-owned assets are in the manufacturing sector.

3   Government of Canada, 1987, pp. 44-45.

Table 12
Foreign Direct Investment in Mexico
(Millions of U.S. Dollars)

Year	New Investment	Accumulated Investment
1979	810.0	6,836.2
1980	1,622.6	8,458.8
1981	1,701.1	10,159.9
1982	626.5	10,786.4
1983	683.7	11,470.1
1984	1,442.2	12,899.9
1985	1,870.1	14,682.9
1986	2,424.2	17,053.1
1987	3,877.2	20,930.3
1988	3,157.1	24,087.4
1989	2,475.4	26,562.8

Source: United States International Trade Commission, Publication 2275, 1990, p. 5-1.

Most of the laws affecting FDI in Mexico stem from the 1917 Constitution. Subsoil resources belonged to the nation, and foreigners were prohibited from owning land in restricted zones. The Law to Promote Mexican Investment and Regulate Foreign Investment (LFI) was promulgated in 1973. It brought together all of the preceding laws and regulations and is in force to this day. Together with the Technical Transfer Law (1973) and the Law of Inventions and Trademarks (1976), it is used to regulate foreign investment and the licensing and sale of foreign industrial property and technology.[4]

Under the relevant legislation, the Mexican economy was divided into four categories:

1. Activities reserved exclusively for the Mexican state, most notably including petroleum and natural gas production, production of basic petrochemicals, railroads, and radio communication;
2. Activities reserved exclusively for Mexicans or for corporations with an exclusive-of-foreigners clause in their articles of incorporation. Prominent sectors here include radio and television and transportation;

4 The following discussion is largely taken from United States International Trade Commission, 1990.

3.   Activities to which foreign investment was subject to specific percentage limitations including mining under concessions and production of automotive parts;
4.   All remaining activities.

The LFI stipulates that foreign investment must not exceed 49 percent of capital and that foreign participation in management cannot be greater than the percent of its investment. Exceptions to this rule could be given by the National Foreign Investment Commission (CNIE). The latter regulates foreign direct investment and approves or rejects projects according to certain criteria. Guidelines issued in 1984 by CNIE liberalized the environment for foreign direct investment by allowing majority foreign participation in various categories of industrial activity, including electrical and non-electrical machinery and equipment, machine tools, transportation equipment, chemical products, biotechnology, and hotels. The requirement to increase Mexican participation within a given time period was also eliminated for these sectors. A related resolution was the elimination of CNIE approval for maquiladora investments. Since the 1984 guidelines were not published, they cannot be considered as an official change in regulations; however, they do reflect a change in policy.

A 1988 General Resolution further liberalized the investment environment by permitting foreign investors to acquire up to 49 percent of the shares of an established Mexican company without prior CNIE approval. If 49 percent of a company was previously held by foreign investors, 100 percent could be acquired without prior approval.

Most recently, The Regulations of the Law to Promote Mexican Investment and Regulate Foreign Investment (May 1989 Regulations), while leaving the LFI in effect, cancels all previous regulations and decrees. Most importantly, it provides standardized rules and requirements for foreign direct investment. The highlights of the published May 1989 regulations include:
1.   Automatic approval of 100 percent foreign investment for certain unclassified activities;
2.   Automatic approval of investment applications after 45 days if no answer is received from CNIE;
3.   Temporary allowance (for up to 20 years) of 100 percent investment through a trust mechanism in classified activities;
4.   Allowance for expansion of existing foreign investments without specific authorization under certain conditions.

In summary, significant liberalization of restrictions on inward foreign direct investment have been undertaken by Mexico since 1984. As an illustration, there were 2,231 foreign-owned capital projects initiated in 1989, and only 213 required prior CNIE approval. Nevertheless, these 213 projects accounted for approximately half the value of all foreign-owned projects initiated in 1989.

Moreover, a long list of industries remain classified, and majority foreign ownership continues to be prohibited in important sectors such as banking and other credit institutions, insurance, communications, most transportation, automobiles, and broadcasting. Petroleum and natural gas exploration, petroleum refining, and the production of basic chemicals remain activities exclusively reserved to the Mexican state.

Maquiladoras

The Maquiladora Program (MP) began in 1965 and was intended to encourage the establishment of export-oriented industries along the Mexican-U.S. border. Maquiladora industries are "in-bond" industries for which raw materials and components can be imported by maquiladora operators duty free. They are then transformed or assembled for export. U.S. imports from maquiladoras pay duty only on the value added in Mexico. Initially, the maquiladoras were primarily in the textile industry. While textile maquiladoras remain prominent in the total, the electrical goods, transportation equipment, and furniture industries are also important.

The maquiladoras are controlled by the Ministry of Industrial Development (SECOFI). SECOFI issues a maquiladora licence which permits the duty-free import of intermediate goods and raw materials. Maquiladoras can be foreign-owned or Mexican owned. Since the inception of the MP, 100 percent foreign ownership has been allowed. Maquiladoras can locate anywhere except the major urban areas of Mexico City, Guadalajara, and Monterrey. Moreover, since August 1983, 20 percent of maquiladora production can be sold in the Mexican market. Over the past few years, measures have been taken by the Mexican government to reduce the time and paperwork necessary to make application and receive approval.

The Treatment of Labour

The existing treatment of nationals from one country seeking to work in another country is a complex process to describe, as it depends, among other things, upon the nature of the work involved, the individual's qualifications, and so forth. Suffice to say that visa requirements and other qualifications stand as barriers to the mobility of labour across national borders, and that labour certification tests and other procedures of similar effect can be and are used to restrict both the temporary and the long-term hiring of foreign nationals across a wide range of occupations.

The FTA takes a step toward alleviating barriers to labour mobility in Article 1501 which articulates the desirability of facilitating temporary entry on a reciprocal basis and of establishing transparent criteria and procedures for temporary entry. The Parties agreed to liberalize national laws and regulations